The Challenge
of Development in the Eighties

Our Response

Other Titles of Interest

BALASSA, B.
Policy Reform in Developing Countries

COLE, S.
Global Models and the International Economic Order

COREA, G.
Need for Change: Towards the New International Economic Order

FRANKO, L. G. & WEIBER, M. J.
Developing Country Debt

MENON, B. P.
Global Dialogue

SAUVANT, K.
Changing Priorities on the International Agenda

STREETEN, P. & JOLLY, R.
Recent Issues in World Development

UNECE
Factors of Growth and Investment Policies

A Related Journal*

WORLD DEVELOPMENT
The multidisciplinary international journal devoted to the
study and promotion of world development.
Chairman of the Editorial Board:
Dr. Paul Streeten, Center for Asian Development Studies,
Boston University, USA

*Free specimen copy available on request.

DROUGHT IN UPPER VOLTA

Credit: UNITED NATIONS/FAO   Photograph by F. Botts

The Challenge
of Development in the Eighties
Our Response

edited by

ANTHONY JENNINGS
Leicester University, U.K.

and

THOMAS G. WEISS
*United Nations Conference on Trade and Development (UNCTAD),
Geneva, Switzerland*

PERGAMON PRESS

OXFORD · NEW YORK · TORONTO · SYDNEY · PARIS · FRANKFURT

U.K.   Pergamon Press Ltd., Headington Hill Hall,
                        Oxford OX3 0BW, England

U.S.A.   Pergamon Press Inc., Maxwell House, Fairview Park,
                        Elmsford, New York 10523, U.S.A.

CANADA   Pergamon Press Canada Ltd., Suite 104,
                        150 Consumers Rd., Willowdale, Ontario M2J 1P9, Canada

AUSTRALIA   Pergamon Press (Aust.) Pty. Ltd., P.O. Box 544,
                        Potts Point, N.S.W. 2011, Australia

FRANCE   Pergamon Press SARL, 24 rue des Ecoles,
                        75240 Paris, Cedex 05, France

FEDERAL REPUBLIC   Pergamon Press GmbH, 6242 Kronberg-Taunus,
OF GERMANY   Hammerweg 6, Federal Republic of Germany

First edition 1982

Library of Congress Cataloging in Publication Data
Main entry under title:
The Challenge of development in the eighties.
1. Economic development—Addresses, essays,
lectures. 2. International economic relations—
Addresses, essays, lectures. I. Jennings,
Anthony, MA. II. Weiss, Thomas George.
HD82.C438   1982   338.9'009'048   82-348
AACR2

British Library Cataloguing in Publication Data

The Challenge of development in the eighties.
1. Underdeveloped areas - Economic conditions
I. Jennings, Anthony II. Weiss, Thomas G.
330.9172'4   HC59.7
ISBN 0-08-027410-2

In order to make this volume available as economically and as rapidly as possible the authors' typescripts have been reproduced in their original forms. This method unfortunately has its typographical limitations but it is hoped that they in no way distract the reader.

Printed in Great Britain by A. Wheaton & Co. Ltd., Exeter

Contents

Contents

Introduction. Background and Purpose of the Book

A. JENNINGS and T. G. WEISS

Economic and social development in the poor nations of the world, which contain the vast majority of the human population, has been unacceptably slow; and the principal reason is the asymmetry prevailing in their relations with the rich industrial world. Acting mainly through the General Assembly of the United Nations, more than 130 developing countries are demanding an equal opportunity to prosper and to participate in the global economy. This demand does not appear unreasonable in conceptual terms; its realisation, however, would amount to nothing less than a radically restructured world economy, overcoming the entrenched interests of the present power structure. Scepticism and moroseness characterize the relationship between developed and developing countries at the beginning of the Third Development Decade. Meaningful dialogue is lacking.

As citizens of the wealthy portion of the globe attempting to understand the demands of developing countries in order to render the present world order more equitable and habitable for all, the contributors to the present volume address their compatriots in developed countries. The editors of the present book have included contributions from as many perspectives as possible — be they academic or practical, from the public or private sectors — so that the breadth of possible perspectives on the process of development could be aired.

In this regard, one must recall that development, like a painting, has quite separate meanings for different observers. No attempt has been made to agree upon an adequate definition or to expand upon the obvious fact that it does not mean the same thing to an OECD planner and a Nepalese peasant. The mosaic of contributions collectively expresses a variety of perspectives and potential support from developed countries to the most challenging and

1

significant human challenge for the remainder of the twentieth
century: creating the conditions that will provide for the
accelerated and sustained economic development of the vast
majority of the human population living in developing countries.
Creating an alternative world order is not only desirable in
terms of basic human justice but also because it can cure the
stagflation in which the industrialized countries have become
mired.

This volume does not aim at sophisticated academic analysis,
but rather it seeks to present the response of different sections of society to the challenge of development in the eighties
in easily understood terms. Our response is not a uniform one,
nor is it immutable. The variety of views reflects that, above
all, development is not static but rather is part of an evolving,
dynamic process. The confrontation of views in this volume will
be useful not only to professionals in education or government
concerned with development, but also to the general public in
their capacities as citizens, trade-unionists, business-persons
and church-goers. This book — and reactions to it — thus provide a forum in which representatives of different interest
groups assess their contribution to the development effort in
the eighties.

In overall terms, what are the objectives of poorer countries in
the 1980s? What is it exactly that citizens of wealthy countries are being asked to consider? Perhaps the best answer to
these questions is found in the recently negotiated text for
the ten-year period that began on 1 January 1981:

"The new International Development Strategy aims at the promotion of the economic and social development of the developing countries with a view to reducing significantly the current
disparities between the developed and developing countries,
as well as the early eradication of poverty and dependency,
which, in turn, would contribute to the solution of international economic problems and sustained global economic
development, and would also be supported by such development
on the basis of justice, equality and mutual benefit. The
International Development Strategy is a vast undertaking involving the entire international community for the promotion
of international development co-operation."

What is required from the general public in wealthy countries
in order to realize such aims? Once again, the text of the new
International Development Strategy for the Third United Nations
Development Decade can be cited:

"It is essential to mobilize public opinion in all countries
and particularly in the developed countries, in order to
obtain their full commitment to the goals and objectives and
to the implementation of the present Strategy. Recognizing
the important role of legislative bodies in contributing to
realistic preparation and effective implementation of national
economic and social development plans, the support of members
of legislative bodies will be essential for the implementation
of the International Development Strategy."

After this brief introduction, seven chapters follow in which
representatives of different interest groups assess their own
perspectives and motivations as well as their possible contributions to the range of development problems. In the concluding
remarks, the editors seek to draw the lessons from the views
expressed.

Chapter 1 is *The Development Decades — Promises, Performance
and Proposals*, written by *Richard Jolly* who is the Director of
the Institute of Development Studies at the University of Sussex.
This article, written by a long-time participant in field
activities as well as an analyst within the United Nations and
the academic world, is particularly important in providing a
general context for subsequent contributions. Professor Jolly
states that "The idea of a development decade is one of those
good ideas which if it did not exist would need to be invented".
He goes on to explain and evaluate the historical importance of
the guidelines, or strategies — that have emerged in the last
20 years. He concludes by giving his views on how those that
have just been agreed for the current decade can be made to
work based on the conviction — shared by almost all other contributors to the present volume — that there must be "a change
of attitude to accept that there are important areas of interest
in achieving a more balanced pattern of world development and
that the North and the socialist bloc have a serious stake in
this, as well as the South".

Chapter 2 is the *Third World's Views of the New International
Development Strategy and the Third Development Decade*, written
by *Thomas G. Weiss* who is presently a member of the secretariat
of the United Nations Conference on Trade and Development
(UNCTAD) in Geneva. He outlines the very unpropitious circumstances in which developing and developed countries have
launched upon the negotiation, and implementation, of the text
to guide governments during the 1980s. He interprets for his
compatriots in the northern developed countries the significance
of the demands for change by their countries found in the new

International Development Strategy.

Chapter 3 is entitled *EC Policy and the Third Development Decade* and was written by *Klaus von Hellsdorff* from the Directorate General for Development and Co-operation of the Commission of the European Communities in Brussels. His starting point is Europe's special responsibility for development as a result of colonisation and its unique response to the challenge of development represented by the two Lomé Conventions. Mr von Hellsdorf argues that these go much farther than the bilateral policies of individual European donors in institutionalizing the Community's development practices on a basis of equality and mutual respect with its partners in developing countries. He speculates about how EC policy toward the developing countries of Asia, the Caribbean and the Pacific could, and should, evolve during the next decade.

Chapter 4 is a discussion of *British Government Policy and the Third Development Decade*. The disparity of views about development, even within the Conservative majority, are quite obvious from the two selections in this chapter: *Government Policy in the Eighties* by the *Right Honourable Neil Marten*, the Minister of Overseas Development, and *An Alternative Conservative View* and response by *Stephen Dorrell*, Secretary of the Conservative Party's Foreign and Commonwealth Affairs Committee. The latter, who is also the youngest Member of Parliament, argues for an active involvement of the United Kingdom in all development issues in the Eighties. In his view, this position reflects the mainstream of the conservative tradition that began with Benjamin Disraeli. His position contrasts distinctly with Mr Marten's one of retrenchment. The Minister argues strongly for an inward-looking position emphasizing the necessity to attack inflation and restore buoyant growth in the United Kingdom and the western world as a means to contribute to development. He also wishes to encourage trade and stimulate private flows of investment to developing countries. Further, because fewer public resources will be devoted to concessionary assistance, the Minister stresses their correct distribution to the poorest countries and to those whose political and economic links with the United Kingdom are the strongest.

Chapter 5 consists of *Management and the Third Development Decade* which was submitted by *Kenneth Durham*, the Vice-Chairman of Unilever Ltd. in London. His own experience with private enterprise's performance in a variety of developing countries has been extremely positive in generating wealth, training local

staff and transferring updated technology. He argues that
"private enterprise companies and particularly, by nature of
their structure and knowledge, the multinational corporations,
will be the most effective agencies for achieving what we all
desire — a significant increase in the well-being of all the
less-well-off nations". Mr Durham argues that multinational
corporations are far more capable of wealth generation than are
international bureaucracies.

Chapter 6 includes two separate analyses of the possible roles
for Trades Unions and the Third Development Decade. *The
Contribution of Trade Unions to Third World Development in the
1980s* was written by *Jack Jones*, the former chairman of the
Trades Union Congress's International Affairs Committee and
General Secretary of the Transport and General Workers Union.
Although Mr Jones is rather more known for his defence of union
interests within the United Kingdom, since his retirement he has
increasingly become involved in the links between workers'
problems in developed and developing countries. He argues that
the development debate must become a popular issue and cease to
occur only in the 'rarified atmosphere' of elites like the Brandt
Commission. He believes that there is more support for increased
aid among the general public than in official government circles
and that steps should be taken to mobilize this latent potential.
In concrete terms, Mr Jones argues that 'grass roots' contacts
between workers from developed and developing countries could
be quite worthwhile in terms of appropriate vocational training
as well as of transferring relevant experiences of health and
safety standards.

Carl Wright, the Director of the Commonwealth Trade Union
Council has written the second part of Chapter 6, *Trade Unions
and Global Development*. He argues for the analytical parallel
between union/management struggles within developed countries
and the negotiations between developing and developed countries
concerning the establishment of an alternative distribution of
labour and a more equitable distribution of the benefits of
growth. As with working people who have refused to accept their
fate and have clamoured for a new economic and social order within national societies, developing countries are now demanding
their fair share. Mr Wright laments that "the attitudes of
certain advanced country governments when faced with the demands
of poor countries, seem to display the same unyielding and
narrow sighted inflexibility that the landed gentry and industrialists of the nineteenth century displayed to the early trade
unions".

Chapter 7 is an attempt to define the particular contribution of Christians in developed countries, *Christians and the Third Development Decade*. Contributors are: *The Archbishop of Canterbury, the Right Reverend R. Runcie; The Archbishop of Westminster, Cardinal B. Hume; and Barbara Ward*. Archbishop Runcie opens Chapter 7 with a discussion of *Christianity and Global Development*. He describes the emergence of global development as a concept central to the Christian view of the world, and he states that the cry of impoverished people is not for charity. It is for justice.

Cardinal Hume pursues this argument in *Churches and the Third Development Decade*. He proposes to study six problems that militate against Christian values in order to devote maximum energy to their removal: the disparity of wealth between nations; the degradation of the physical environment; the failure to control energy use; the potentially catastrophic effects of nuclear war; widespread hunger; and the failure to respect the rights of the individual. Labelling these six threats a "collective sin", Cardinal Hume proposes that Christians discover in Christ the new ideas and the necessary inspiration to work for significant social change.

The final article in the chapter is Barbara Ward's *The Third Development Decade: A Christian Responds*. Known across the world for her professional economic analyses, Barbara Ward reveals the source of strength underlying her personal commitment to work on development: Her action as a Christian to the great issue of international social justice "must inevitably be rooted in the Gospel and the words of Christ". Buttressing her convictions with the findings of the Brandt Commission, she argues forcibly for a 'global Marshall Plan' during the eighties. Systematically increasing the purchasing power and skills of the poor could act as an 'engine of growth' to stop intolerable levels of unemployment and the steady rise in inflationary pressure in the Western World. We are sad to note that this is one of Barbara Ward's last contributions before her death. The Third World cause has lost one of its most eloquent and compassionate champions.

The editors of this book are proud to have responsibility for putting together such a disparate and impressive collection of essays on the challenge of development during the forthcoming ten-year period. A word of gratitude is in order for the Commission for International Justice and Peace of the Roman Catholic Bishop's Conference of England and Wales. Under their auspices, a colloquium on 'Britain and the Third Development Decade' was organized at Westminster in March 1980. Most of the papers in the present volume were originally presented at this meeting. The proceeds from the present book will be used by the CIJP to foster a continuing dialogue about development in the eighties.

Geneva, Switzerland
January 1981
                                    Anthony Jennings
                                    Thomas G. Weiss

CHAPTER 1

The Development Decades —
Promises, Performance and
Proposals

RICHARD JOLLY

In principle, the idea of a development decade has enormous
relevance for the 1980s. The world economy languishes in recession and stagflation. It is also increasingly interdependent,
with inflation, recession and possibilities of recovery progress
in any one country depending not only on its own policies and
actions but also on the collective impact of the policies and
actions of all other countries. An endless series of meetings
and negotiations, bilateral and multilateral, regional and
international, take place each year which attempt to bring
greater harmony to these policies and actions. Generally,
however, such interactions are themselves largely uncoordinated,
confused and lacking in vision, taking up issues as they arise,
usually within a short- to medium term framework. They make
limited, if any, reference to long term goals within individual
countries, let alone goals for development within the world
economy. Would it not help if, in contrast, the world community
could agree on a few high priority goals and objectives, agreed
to be in the mutual interests of the countries concerned, which
could then set a long term framework of changes required and
goals to be achieved?

In these terms — and if governments were prepared to make
effective commitments, a point I shall come to later — it seems
difficult not to agree with the idea of a development decade.
It would *not* be, nor attempt to be, a comprehensive world
development plan, but rather 'a practical set of goals for
providing a more favourable world economic environment for
development'.[1]

---

[1]Committee for Development Planning: *Report on 16th Session,*
January 1980, ECOSOC official records 1980, Supplement No 2,

9

Yet a development decade is a good idea which so far has worked
only badly or not at all. The former Director-General of
Swedish Aid, who was a close participant in the formulation of
the first two Development Decades, recently wrote: "I can see
nothing that could reasonably be said to prove, or make likely,
the fact that the United Nations international development
strategies have influenced actual world development in the 1960s
and the 1970s. Possibly, their strategies have contributed to
the disappointment, particularly with the UN system, that now
exists in many quarters. Probably, they have been of little
consequence because they remain largely unknown."[2]

Is this a fair assessment — and must this be the inevitable out-
come for the future?

ORIGINS OF THE FIRST DEVELOPMENT DECADE
AND SUBSEQUENT DEVELOPMENTS

The occasion for proposing the First Development Decade (DDI)
was more political than economic. Shortly after his inauguration
as President of the United States in January 1961, John F.
Kennedy visited the General Assembly in New York, aiming to
inspire the international debate with the same image of youthful
dynamism and purpose that he had brought to the US presidency.
Mankind was to reach the moon before the end of the decade.
Kennedy proposed also a development decade in which mankind
would take a decisive step towards the eradication of poverty,
illiteracy and hunger.

UN New York, para 11 (hereafter referred to as CDP 1980). This
is, of course, only one possible view of a development decade.
Professor Jan Tinbergen, first Chairman of the CDP believed
that the second Development Decade ought to become a World
Indicative Plan. Others have thought this overambitious and
unrealistic. See 'Planning a New Strategy', pp 71-76, in
Colin Legum (ed) *The First UN Development Decade and its Lessons
for the 1970s* (Praeger, New York, 1970). The CDP report was
subsequently published under the title *Shaping Accelerated
Development and International Change* (United Nations, New York,
1980, ST/ESA/105.

[2] Ernst Michanek, 'The Strategy Smokescreen', *Development Forum*,
Nov-Dec 1979, p 1.

A few days later, a formal proposal was put to the General
Assembly by a group of countries headed by the United States,
which, with various additions and amendments, was approved by
the General Assembly in December 1961 as resolution 1710 (XIV).
This not only set out the goals of the decade, but set a pattern
for thinking about decades which has largely continued until
the present.

The main objective of DDI was to 'accelerate progress towards
self-sustaining growth of the economy of the individual nations
and their social advancement so as to attain in each underdeveloped country a substantial increase in the rate of economic
growth. Each country would set its own target, taking as the
objective a minimum rate of growth of aggregate national income
of 5 per cent at the end of the decade'. 'Progress towards
self-sustaining growth' was a direct echo of Rostow's take-off
theory and of the rationale, then current, of international aid
as a short-term boost to enable countries to reach a level of
growth which would be sustainable without inflows of aid or
private capital from abroad.

Although 'take-off' is no longer in vogue, self-sustaining
growth under the broader concept of self-reliance is still
highly contemporary. However, the early emphasis on 'each
country setting its own target' is, in my view, a highly desirable feature of the early strategy which has in part been lost.
It reflected the greater optimism at that time about the realism
of national planning — and this may now rightly be approached
with greater caution. But it also indicated the need, if a
global strategy were to be meaningful, for its main goals to be
related to declared national objectives and targets — a link
which DDII attempted to make even more closely but failed
through lack of country support.

Early in 1962, the UN secretariat prepared a fuller document,
'Proposals for Action',[3] drawing on all of the specialised UN
agencies in order to elaborate what the goals might mean in the
areas of human resources, sectoral development, international
trade, development financing, technical co-operation and other
aids to development and planning. These proposals were considered and accepted by the Economic and Social Council (ECOSOC)
in mid-1962 and a special committee on co-ordination established

---

[3]Hans Singer was the main author, to whom I am grateful for
much of the information for this section of the paper.

to review UN activities related to the Decade and to propose
priority projects and areas for action.

Preparation for the Second Development Decade was different.
In 1966, a Committee on Development Planning (CDP) was created
under the chairmanship of Jan Tinbergen, initially to monitor
progress during the First Decade, later to make proposals for
the Second. A Preparatory Committee of government representatives was established in 1968. Even to have a Second Development
Decade was itself an innovation: the First Decade was conceived
as a ten-year effort, not the first of a series of such decades,
which later it became. The CDP prepared its proposals in the
form of a report, *Towards Accelerating Development,* which later
became the main part of the documentation for the General
Assembly at its 25th Session at the end of 1970. The United
Nations resolutions for the Second Development Decade were
agreed as *International Development Strategy: an Action Programme of the General Assembly for the Second United Nations
Development Decade* issued at the end of 1970, to mark the
twenty-fifth anniversary of the UN System.

By the time of the preparation of the Third Development Decade,
the whole process was more institutionalised and heavily influenced by the UN sixth and seventh Special Sessions which in
1974 and 1975 had proclaimed the need for a New International
Economic Order. In addition, the post of Deputy Secretary-
General within the United Nations had been created, with special
responsibilities for economic and social matters, including the
Third Development Decade.[4] The CDP met to evaluate progress
during DDII and to make recommendations for the DDIII, especially
in its reports of 1979 and 1980.

In parallel, and now politically more important than before, a
Preparatory Committee comprising representatives of all member
governments had been meeting, often sharply divided on general
positions taken on North-South issues. In addition, and formally
outside the UN, the ICIDI or 'Brandt Commission' had been meeting
for two years and submitted its report to the Secretary-General
in February 1980, which was also intended to be a major input
into the Special Session of the UN in August/September 1980.

---

[4]Kenneth Dadzie, the first holder of the post of Director-
General for Development at International Economic Co-operation,
has elaborated his views on 'Key Elements in the International
Development Strategy' in Khadija Haq, *Dialogue for a New Order*
(Pergamon, New York, 1980).

DDI AND DDII — GOALS AND OBJECTIVES

It has become customary to describe the goals of the DDI as
totally preoccupied with growth to the neglect of issues of
distribution and structural change. In fact, both the 1961 UN
resolution and its elaboration in the Proposals for Action are
much broader, stressing that 'development is not just economic
growth, it is growth plus change'.[5] An acceleration of the
growth of incomes was certainly emphasized to be a critical
part of the strategy, with the target of developing countries
as a group attaining a rate of growth of GNP of 5 per cent per
annum by the end of the Decade. In the event, this goal was
more than achieved. Developing countries as a group averaged
a growth rate of 5.9 per cent in real terms over the whole
period from 1960-1970, well above the targeted rate for the end
of the decade. Not surprisingly, the target growth rate for
DDII was raised to 6 per cent, with the Chairman of the CDP,
Professor Tinbergen, pressing for a higher rate and with the
rider that the poorer countries should achieve a rate in excess
of this.

Quantitative targets were also suggested for the growth of *per
capita* output, agricultural and manufacturing output, exports,
imports and the rate of savings.

Table 1 sets out the basic quantitative goals together with the
actual rates achieved for DDI and DDII. By the naive test of
achievement in relation to target, Table 1 suggests that both
decades ought to be given high marks. The central goal of income growth was more than achieved during DDI and only slightly
underachieved in DDII — averaging, over both Decades taken together, slightly above the target. If these results were
achieved in any national plan, politicians would be boasting
great success.

In fact, of course, such results are highly misleading. In the
first place, the goals and achievements are averages, lumping
together performance in well over 100 countries and thus dis-
guising vast differences of performance. Over both Decades, and
in the 1970s especially, average results combine well above
average growth-rate performance in the richer developing
countries, the OPEC countries and those with thriving exports
like the newly industrializing countries (NICs), and markedly

---

[5]Proposals for Action, (v).

Table 1

MAIN QUANTITATIVE GOALS OF DDI, DDII and DDIII WITH ACTUAL AND
ESTIMATED PERFORMANCE OVER DDI AND DDII
(all figures percentages)

Country group and item:	DDI Target	DDI Performance 1960-1970	DDII Target	DDII Performance 1970-1978	DDIII Targets
Growth rates of GDP (% increase per year)					
GDP total developing countries	to reach 5.0 by 1970	5.9	6	5.5	7
low income countries[a]	more than 5[b]	4.2	more than 6	3.2	7
Per capita GDP growth (% increase per year)					
total developing countries	1.5-2.5[b]	3.4	3.5	2.8	4.5
low income countries	–	1.8	more than 3.5	0.6	–
Agricultural output (% increase per year)	4-4.5[b]	3.8	4	2.9	4
Manufacturing output (% increase per year)	9.0[b]	7.7	8	6.8	9
Resource transfers as shares of GNP of economically advanced countries					
Net total financial resource transfers	to reach and maintain 1%		1	1	–
Net official development assistance		0.7	0.7	0.3	0.7 by 1985 or during 1986-1989

(a) Low income countries are those with GDP *per capita* of less than US$300 in 1975(and in 1975 prices).

(b) strictly these were not recommended targets but implications stated in the Proposals for Action.

Source: Column 1 — United Nations, *The UN Development Decade: Proposals for Action*, UN, New York, 1962.
 Column 2 — World Bank, Tables 1976 & *World Development Report* 1979.
 Columns 3 + 4 — Annexe 1, CDP Report on 16th Session 1980.
 Column 5 — Figures from United Nations A/35/464 Annexe

below average performance in the low-income countries which
account for two-thirds of the total Third World population.
The averaging of such disparate experience has led many people
to conclude, in the words of the 1979 CDP report, that:

"The very fact that the Second Development Decade target of
6 per cent annual growth in gross domestic product for the
developing countries as a whole is likely to be almost
achieved over the 1970s has underlined the inadequacy of such
an aggregative global target."[6]

In the second place, growth-rate performance is misleading
because growth by itself is not development. Indeed, in many
developing countries, with inadequate statistics and rapid inflation, the recorded growth of GNP may not even be actual
growth, since both the raw data and the 'deflators' used for
estimating real growth rates are often highly unreliable.
Furthermore, the statistics on production and incomes in most
economies of Africa and in many of Asia, Latin America and the
Middle East refer to the 'modern sector' ignoring or making
only rough and patchy estimates of rural production and incomes
and the small-scale and informal urban sector. Yet these are
the sectors on which the majority of the population depend for
their incomes and welfare. Even in the fast-growing countries —
OPEC countries and the NICs, in particular — growth rates can
be highly misleading, since so many other aspects of living
standards and national development are not included, and may
even deteriorate in periods of very rapid 'growth'.

Growth-rate goals are also inadequate for more technical
reasons. Being averages across countries, they give too little
weight to performance in the larger and poorer developing
countries, where populations number two-thirds of the total
Third World population. By concentrating on total income
growth, such goals may overestimate *per capita* growth, as
occurred during DDI, especially in the low-income countries,
where population grew faster than was originally estimated and
per capita income increased by under 2 per cent per annum.
Over the 1970s, *per capita* income in the low-income countries
increased by only about one-half per cent per annum. Finally,
targets expressed as growth rates over a decade tend to imply
a steady process of growth, which sharply contrasts with the
fluctuations and stop-start performance which was typical rather

---

[6]*CDP* 1979, p 1.

than exceptional in the 1970s and which afflicted many individual countries even in the 1960s. In view of this reality it is
not surprising that the relatively good quantitative performance
on paper must be judged to be extremely misleading, casting more
doubts on the relevance of the targets than on the apparent
success of their achievement.

As stressed earlier, however, many non-quantitative goals were
in fact included in both DDI and DDII, though forgotten or un-
derplayed in their later evaluation. Was performance in respect
of these more qualitative goals any better? A major difficulty
in answering the question is the diversity and imprecision of
the goals in question. Both DDI and DDII identified a wide
range of issues, domestic and international, with which the
Decade should be concerned: food and nutrition, housing, education, literacy, health and infant mortality. In fact all the
conventional components of today's 'basic needs' were fore-
shadowed. Structural change in land tenure, income distribution
and participation were also emphasised, as well as the need to
increase employment, and special measures to achieve an increase
in the incomes of the poorest sections of the population.

Internationally, the range of proposals was also very large.
A great deal of attention was given to trade, emphasising the
need for stable and remunerative prices in expanding markets,
for equitable shares of earnings from the extraction and marketing of natural resources by foreign capital, as well as for
commodity agreements, easier access to developed country markets
and increasing proportions of processing to be undertaken within
producing countries. Increased capital flows, both public and
private, increased technology, and channelling savings from
disarmament into international development were clearly mentioned. In all these respects, the documents for the 1960s,
1970s and 1980s are perhaps more similar than many persons now
realise. If the cover were missing, it would not be easy to
tell whether one was reading a draft prepared a few months ago
or 20 years earlier.

Yet there are some important differences of philosophy and
approach, not just of nuance. The DDI documents see the development problem almost entirely in terms of building domestic
capacity within developing countries to achieve self-sustained
growth in the longer run — with local savings and capital inflows
being the critical contributions to physical investment, and
local education and training and technical assistance being the
critical contribution to human investment. As mentioned earlier,
one can also discern the intellectual origins of the first

Development Decade in Rostow's 'take-off model' where countries develop by raising their net savings ratios to the point where they reach take-off and self-sustaining growth.

The DDII documents reveal more awareness of unequal relation-ships — in technology and shipping, for instance — and the need for special measures in favour of the least developed and land-locked among the developing countries, to offset the persistent bias in the world economic system against such countries. The most recent reports of the CDP and the 1979-1980 debates of the Preparatory Committee and the draft text of DDIII[7] show even greater concern with 'asymmetries, inequities and imbalances' in a whole range of international economic relationships and a clear emphasis on the need for international change in these respects as well as international support for developing countries in their national efforts to develop. The intellec-tual models underlying these more recent developments are more diverse and there is clear influence from structural and dependency analysis.

DDI AND DDII — PERFORMANCE

Taking account of this wide range of goals, a simple summation of performance is difficult. At one extreme, one is asking for an evaluation of almost the whole of development experience over the last two decades in some way which can be measured against the perceptions as well as the formal goals of the UN documents. At the other, one is asking for an evaluation of how much of this development, or the changes of policy, struc-ture and institutions can be attributed to the Development Decades as such. Either evaluation is virtually impossible, and certainly so in only a few pages. As regards the second type of evaluation, however, one may note the generally pessimistic views of the effectiveness of the Decades. Although formal texts may state that "the adoption of the International Develop-ment Strategy for the Second United Nations Development Decade was an important step in the promotion of international economic co-operation for development", in private, those closely involved are more cautious and often sceptical.[8]

---

[7]The International Development Strategy for the Third United Nations Development Decade, A/35/464 of 23 October 1980, here-after referred to as UN-IDS-DDIII.

[8]Quote from UN-IDS-DDIII preamble.

A working group of the CDP in 1978 asked what effect, if any,
the earlier Development Decades and their targets had on the
action of governments. They concluded that, in a modest way,
the two Decades had helped to raise awareness of global development issues, had identified and clarified issues in the course
of their preparation (though not always the right issues,
judged by hindsight) and had provided, and could still provide,
a yardstick by which to judge certain international commitments
and performance. Aid was the most specific example of this.
Although on average official development assistance (ODA)
performance has fallen far behind the 0.7 per cent target for
the 1970s, it seemed clear that the above-target performance
of Sweden and Holland and the on-target performance of Norway
and Denmark had been positively influenced by including the 0.7
per cent target as a goal of the Second Development Decade.

The Development Assistance Committee, comprising all the main
donors of the OECD countries, had institutionalised standardised
reporting and regular reviews of aid performance. Both government and non-government groups in these countries had used the
0.7 per cent target to build up popular support for meeting or
exceeding this goal. Such limited and uncertain influence is
a far cry from the grandeur of the long lists of desirable
development goals solemnly approved by governments in the
General Assembly. But in one respect the partial success of
even this one goal may have an important moral. It is the one
goal of the first and second Decades which had direct, specific
and measurable implications for individual country performance,
and where other parts of the world community had a direct interest in its fulfilment. It was thus a goal of genuinely
international concern, and a goal against which the performance
of individual countries could unambiguously be measured. Indeed,
OECD's Development Assistance Committee, monitoring sessions
and annual reviews of development co-operation are important
examples of the institutional developments which have followed
from the goal of expanding aid transfers and increasing their
effectiveness. These characteristics ought to be given greater
prominence in future Decades, and be carried also into other
areas of international performance, especially where there is a
clear element of mutual interest in the achievement of the goals.

THE THIRD DEVELOPMENT DECADE

After nearly two years of often tortuous preparations, a draft
'International Development Strategy for the Third United Nations
Development Decade' was approved by the General Assembly during

its 35th Session at the end of 1980. The text had emerged after
two years of meetings of the Preparatory Committee, much supportive work in the UN secretariat in member delegations and other
groups, and after further meetings during the eleventh special
session of the UN itself.

The text is long — nearly 50 closely-worded pages — compared
with the terse two pages of the First Development Decade. It
contains four sections:

I   Preamble — providing broad perspectives on the Decade,
but identifying certain priorities and key principles
and responsibilities for implementation.

II   Goals and Objectives — summarising the major goals, both
quantifiable targets and broad objectives for accelerating
growth and development in the Third World, including
human and social as well as economic advances.

III   Policy Measures — in the areas of international trade,
industrialisation, food and agiculture, financial resources for development, international monetary and
financial issues, technical co-operation, science and
technology for development, energy, transport, economic
and technical co-operation among developing countries,
environment, human settlements, disaster relief and social
development. In addition, there is an important section
of special policy measures for four groups of countries
with special needs — the least developed, developing
island and land-locked developing countries, and those
most seriously affected by the current economic crisis.

IV   Action for Review and Appraisal of Implementation.

Certain key issues and goals are identified at the very beginning. The current state of structural disequilibrium of the
international economy, with slower growth, high inflation, unemployment and uncertain long term prospects is set alongside
the inequities and imbalances in relations between developed
and developing countries, and the stark reality ... that close
to 850 million people in the developing world are living at the
margin of existence. Accordingly, the International Development
Strategy is seen as 'an integral part of the continuing efforts
of the international community to establish a new international
economic order (NIEO)'.

The use of 'a' rather than 'the' in front of NIEO indicates the

gulf which still divides most of the developed from the developing countries in interpreting even the broad meaning of NIEO,
let alone its possible details and specifics. The strategy
also emphasises the broader human dimensions of development —
the development process must promote human dignity, and a substantial improvement in the status of women — as well as a whole
series of more specific targets in the areas of health, education
and physical wellbeing. The strategy recognises that 'the
primary responsibility for the development of developing countries rests upon those countries themselves'— an obvious truth,
perhaps, but worth underlining for those who feel that an international strategy lets developing countries off the hook (often
a developed country feeling) or opens the way to interference
with the internal affairs of developing countries (often a
developing country fear).

The goals and objectives of the strategy are spelled out at
considerable length — nine pages — with the result that priority
international goals and desirable developments, national or
international, get run together in a listing at times so broad
and comprehensive as to be almost all things to all men, (and,
no doubt, all women and all children besides). The main
quantitative goals have already been summarised in Table 1. A
target growth rate for annual average GDP growth for the developing countries as a whole is fixed at 7 per cent, with the
proviso that each developing country will 'set its own target
for growth in the light of its particular circumstances' and
that 'special efforts are required to ensure that the low-income
developing countries attain the average rate of 7 per cent'.
This goal is enormously ambitious, especially in the context of
continuing world recession in which the Decade begins. It is
even more ambitious for the low-income developing countries,
whose performance in the 1970s averaged less than half this goal.

The goals for structural change in industry, agriculture, energy,
technology and monetary institutions vary enormously in depth
and specificity. In some cases, notably agriculture and world
food security, the positions adopted by the major groups of
countries are not so different and a precise range of fairly
detailed proposals has emerged. In the case of energy, sharp
differences between countries have prevented more than a fairly
conventional list of measures, mainly in support of increased
energy production in non-oil developing countries.

The following is a summary of proposals in three major areas:
goals for the human and social dimensions of development — which
though not new, have been particularly emphasised in the DDIII

strategy; international monetary and financial issues — a vital
area for international reform; and financial resources for development — the area where the goals for donor countries are
most specific.

GOALS FOR THE HUMAN AND SOCIAL DIMENSIONS OF DEVELOPMENT

(1) *The reduction and elimination of poverty and a fair dis-*
     tribution of the benefits of development are primary objec-
     tives for the international community during the Decade.

(2) *The attainment of full employment* by the year 2000 remains
     a primary objective.

(3) The international community recognises the need for
     countries to continue to strengthen their implementation
     of the recommendations of the World Population Plan of
     Action — to ensure *the right of parents to determine the*
     number and spacing of their children and make universally
     available advice on and means of achieving the desired
     family size.

(4) *The eradication or considerable reduction of illiteracy*
     and the closest possible realisation of universal primary
     enrolment by the year 2000 remain major goals.

(5) *The attainment by the year 2000 of a level of health that*
     will permit all peoples of the world to lead a socially
     and economically prdouctive life is an important objective
     of the international community. All countries will broaden
     the access of the poorest groups in their populations to
     health facilities and, with the assistance of the inter-
     national community, will ensure immunisation against major
     infectious diseases for all children as early as possible
     during the Decade.

(6) *Safe water and adequate sanitary facilities* should also be
     made available to all in rural and urban areas by 1990.

(7) *The reduction of mortality rates* will be a major objective.
     In the poorest countries, infant mortality should be reduced
     to less than 120 per 1000 live births. Life expectancy in
     all countries should reach 60 years as a minimum, and

infant mortality rates should reach 50 per 1000 live births,
as a maximum, by the year 2000.

(8)   Particular efforts should be made to *integrate the disabled
      in the development process.* Effective measures of preven-
      tion and rehabilitation are therefore essential.

(9)   *The provision of basic shelter and infrastructure for all
      people, in rural as well as urban areas,* is a long term
      goal ... including greater benefits to low-income groups.

(10) Full and effective participation by the entire population
      at all stages of the development process should be ensured.

INTERNATIONAL MONETARY AND FINANCIAL ISSUES

Further reform of the international monetary and financial systems should be pursued and carried out expeditiously early in
and throughout the Decade. The principal features of a stable,
effective and equitable system should include:

(1)   *an effective, symmetrical and equitable adjustment process*
      consistent with high sustainable employment and growth,
      price stability and the dynamic expansion of world trade.
      Effective adjustment requires access to official credit
      facilities on terms and conditions adapted to the nature
      of the balance of payments problems of the countries
      concerned.

(2)   *the terms and conditions of existing IMF facilities, in-
      cluding the compensatory financing facility, to be reviewed
      periodically,* to ensure that they are adequate and adapted
      to member country needs and coping adequately with changing
      world economic conditions. The Fund should conclude at an
      early date its consideration of mechanisms to reduce the
      cost of using the supplementary financing facility.

(3)   *assistance to countries, especially developing countries,
      with structural imbalance in their external accounts,* in-
      cluding immediate action to improve collaboration between
      the IMF and the World Bank, particularly as regards
      medium-term balance of payments financing. Consideration
      should be given *inter alia* to the need for additional

resources, to the conditionality attached to those resources, to the maturity periods involved and to measures
to reduce the cost of borrowing for low-income developing
countries.

(4) *the reduction of inflation and the restoration of high
     sustainable growth,* a stable yet sufficiently flexible
     exchange rate system, with equitable and symmetrical
     treatment by the IMF of surplus and deficit countries in
     exercising its surveillance and the creation of inter-
     national liquidity through collective international action.

(5) *the establishment of a link between SDRs and development
     assistance.*

(6) *provision by the IMF for equitable and effective partici-
     pation of developing countries in IMF decision making.*

FINANCIAL RESOURCES FOR DEVELOPMENT

Developing countries will continue to bear the main responsibility for framing their development and will adopt rigorous
measures for a fuller mobilisation of their domestic financial
resources.

Improved aid performance by developed countries

International financial flows, particularly public flows, should
be improved and adapted consistent with the needs of developing
countries as regards volume, composition, quality forms and distribution of flows. In particular:

(1) bilateral and multilateral *flows will be made on an in-
     creasingly assured, continuous and predictable basis.*

(2) *a rapid and substantial increase will be made in ODA by*
     all developed countries with a view to *reaching and, where
     possible, surpassing the agreed international target of
     0.7 per cent* of the GNP of developed countries. Developed
     countries which have not yet reached the target should
     exert their best efforts to reach it by 1985, and in any
     case not later than the second half of the Decade. The
     target of 1 per cent should be reached as soon as possible
     thereafter.

(3)   *flows of ODA will increasingly be directed towards the
      least-developed countries* and developing countries in the
      other special categories where development needs and prob-
      lems are greatest. Efforts will be made by donor countries
      *to double as soon as possible the flow of ODA to the least-
      developed countries* (LLDCs) — giving consideration not
      later than at the UN Conference on LLDCs in 1981, for
      tripling the net flow of ODA to LLDCs by 1984 and quadrup-
      ling it by 1990 at 1977 prices.

(4)   *donor countries should announce their plans or intentions
      for the longest period ahead and, where possible, for a
      minimum period of three years.*

(5)   *the terms and conditions of ODA should be significantly
      improved;* increasing the current overall average rate of
      conditionality; ODA to LLDCs should as a general rule be
      in the form of grants; ODA should as a general rule be
      untied, and the share of programme assistance and local
      and recurrent cost financing be increased substantially.

(6)   *donor countries will continue to improve their aid-giving
      procedures,* in consultation with the beneficiary countries,
      so as to reduce obstacles to rapid aid disbursements and
      effective aid uses.

International agency flows

*Flows from international and regional development finance
institutions should be increased significantly.* In particular,
agreements reached to increase the capital of the World Bank
and replenish IDA will be speedily implemented. *Ways and means
to achieve long-term financing and multi-year pledging of UN
development assistance programmes should also be considered,*
along with ways and means to strengthen lending capacities of
World Bank and regional development banks by such proposals as
raising their lending-capital ratios.

The World Bank should consider steps for the establishment of
a long-term financing facility to finance the purchase of
capital goods by LDCs.

Non-concessional flows

*Non-concessional flows will continue to be important — and new
and innovative means for increasing such transfers will be ex-
plored,* including such means as cofinancing, multilateral
guarantees for borrowing in international markets, interest

subsidy mechanisms, programme or non-project loans, improved
access to private capital markets. *The UN Secretary General
should examine the proposal for a World Development Fund* and
report to the General Assembly not later than its 36th session.

Debt-relief and balance of payments support

Governments should seek to implement earlier commitments on
debt-relief actions and continue retroactive terms adjustment.

Urgent consideration should be given through the IMF and other
relevant international financial institutions to *special and
favourable criteria for developing countries when they receive
balance of payments support.*

Disarmament

Effective measures should be taken to *use resources released by
disarmament for economic and social development,* particularly
for the benefit of the developing countries.

SOME CRITICAL AND NEGLECTED ISSUES

If the broader range of goals and objectives are seriously
implemented, it would be an important advance on the approaches
of the earlier two decades, especially where these goals relate
to international action in which countries in different parts
of the world have an interest in implementation. Admittedly,
much more would be required for the Development Decades to have
a serious impact on policy and action. Moreover, it would be
misleading not to emphasise the limited extent to which the DDIII
text grapples with some of the problems and weaknesses earlier
identified. Although the text clearly identifies the special
needs of low-income countries, and proposes a doubling of the
national income of this group of countries by the end of the
Decade, this still falls far short of some of the major issues
involved.

The prospects of achieving the 7 per cent growth target for low-
income countries cannot be rated very high, in the light of past
experience. Moreover, although there is recognition of the
special needs of the low-income developing countries, the most
seriously affected, the land-locked and island developing
countries, the ways in which action might respond to their differences has yet to be elaborated. Systematic recognition is,
in my view, also required of the differing needs and economic

strengths of the whole range of developing countries, based on
their general structural differences. This ought to be possible
without violating the need to build and preserve Third World
solidarity in bargaining and negotiations.

Secondly, the strategy still largely concerns long-run changes
over the Decade, in spite of its recognition that recession
and instability are likely to dominate the early years of the
Decade — and perhaps the whole of it, unless effective remedial
measures are taken. Too few of the strategy's components are
strongly or integrally related to ways in which dynamism can be
restored to the international economy and to the specific
actions which both developed and developing countries should
take to achieve this. Integrated proposals, such as those of
the Emergency Programme of the Brandt Report — for a major
transfer of resources to developing countries as a stimulus to
economic activity and to structural change in energy, food production and world economic institutions — are only lightly
touched upon. When the history of 'recession and world economic
disarray in the 1980s' is written, future historians are likely
to decry the failure to make such measures central in the
strategy of the Decade, and to make them a focus of much more
specific debate in the Special Session.

The role of the socialist countries in the strategy is also
almost entirely neglected, save for a final proposal that
'Changes in the international economic system to encourage and
make possible the fuller participation of the countries with
centrally-planned economies in international trade and other
economic relations on the basis of equitable conditions without
discrimination should be a goal of the Third Development Decade,
particularly in ways which help promote the progress of developing countries.' In other words, the world community still has
far to go to construct an approach and a relevant set of international goals for the Decade, which would make it a genuine
forum for effective international action.

HOW TO MAKE IMPLEMENTATION OF DDIII MORE EFFECTIVE

With two Decades of experience behind us, the world community
ought to be ready to consider more frankly amd more seriously
what they believe can be achieved through the present Development Decade, based on a frank and realistic assessment of past
experience. In a casual way, such assessments are made in the
corridors if not the formal assemblies of the UN, if only by a
certain cynical attitude to the meaningfulness of the whole

exercise as presently conducted.

The starting point, in my view, must be with a change of attitude to accept that there are important areas of interest in
achieving a more balanced pattern of world development and that
the North and the socialist bloc have a serious stake in this,
as well as the South. At the moment, in spite of strong statements of the case, most notably by the Brandt Commission, this
is far from being generally or genuinely accepted. Apart from
oil issues and OPEC, the North generally thinks of the North-
South debate as an area for diplomacy and damage limitation,
not as an arena where serious economic goals which could improve
the health of their own economies could be pursued. The socialist bloc usually adopts an even more detached stance, treating
the North-South debate as outside its own concerns. The South
realizes that the issues are critical for its own economic
future, but given so little engagement in serious negotiation
of specific issues, claim gets piled upon claim, with an
escalation of demands, hopes and rhetoric which far exceeds any
feasible agenda for immediate negotiation.

The second main need is to concentrate on a more limited range
of issues on which the main blocs of countries have some serious
interest. The Brandt Commission's report has stressed the need
for this and their Emergency Programme would be a start. The
essential point is that the main groups of countries should
come to the negotiating table with a defined and limited set of
economic objectives which they really wish to achieve — and
which they seriously believe also have something to offer to
the other parties. There is still room for this in the latest
round of global negotiations which started in 1981, in parallel
with launching the Third Development Decade.

It is still not clear what role there is for goals of the
Development Decade in this process. Many would say 'none' —
even those who accept the need for a new start and the two
starting points identified above. This approach is unnecessarily
defeatist, indeed dangerously so. There is urgent need for a
frame for international action and without it, many pressing
problems which can only be tackled by co-ordinated international
action will go unresolved, or be tackled in a totally *ad hoc*
manner. If this happens, as has happened during most of the
past decade and since the breakdown of the Bretton Woods system,
the world economy is likely to continue in disarray, seriously
inhibiting the ability of individual countries to restore
growth, to achieve structural change and to move to a more
steady and successful pattern of development over the next

decade or two. But if treated seriously, the goals for the
Decade could help to give focus for the global round.

There is also the need to work out and agree upon measures to
give more practical effect to the implementation of the Decade,
within the framework of procedures and summarised at the conclusion of the text of the strategy. This suggests various
ways in which the Decade can be made more operational:

— Working out at the regional or sub-regional level the specific
  measures for implementing the main goals of the Decade for
  groups of countries or even individual countries, preferably
  with specific agreement on how they can be achieved. Something along these lines was in fact proposed by the CDP in
  1970 for the General Assembly which would formally approve
  the goals for DDII. It was suggested that each country as a
  minimum should pledge its support for the goals of the Decade,
  but, in addition, indicate further goals or measures that it
  would be prepared to implement on a unilateral basis. The
  idea of such specific national pledges is still relevant and
  might be more feasible if considered at the regional or sub-
  regional level, especially in relation to issues where action
  at this level is directly relevant.

— The CDP has also suggested more recently that action towards
  the Decade could be made more operational by including a
  limited number of regional or global projects whose implementation would form a practical and visible part of the Decade.
  Such projects might include multinational river basin control
  projects, the African regional transport plan, or measures
  for the eradication of major diseases such as river blindness.
  The identification and implementation of such projects could
  do much to bring home to ordinary people the relevance of the
  Decade and the practical value of international co-operation
  to achieve some of its goals.

— The use of DDIII goals for setting basic guidelines for the
  programmes of the various UN agencies is included in the
  strategy and, if carried through in specific terms, would be
  an obvious step towards implementation. This too was suggested for both DDI and DDII, though in the event the goals of
  the Decade seem to have been taken as little more than a
  general endorsement of the basic and continuing programmes of
  the different agencies. Nevertheless, the specific goals
  proposed for DDIII, especially with respect to international
  structural change and the reform of international institutions

and mechanisms, seem well devised to provide more relevant
guidelines for the UN agencies in the future, especially in
the case of the IMF and the World Bank. Here, much could be
achieved if there were continuing serious agreement among the
nations concerned that the UN agencies should give high
priority to supporting the targets along the lines proposed.

— Greater flexibility in the process of monitoring, evaluating
  and subsequently adjusting the goals and specific policies of
  the Decade to achieve greater implementation is required. If
  this were carried out with vision and commitment, the measure
  of flexibility desired could be combined with further agreements for support of the ultimate objectives of the Decade.
  But the obvious reality of this proposal is caught between
  those who argue that a measure of flexibility is necessary
  for realism and those who fear that any measure of flexibility
  will be exploited by those who wish to renegue on earlier
  commitments.

CONCLUSION

Such points are the detail of making the new international
development strategy really effective. The primary issue is for
the major governments to accept that co-ordinated international
action is an important part of the solution to their own economic
and social problems and thus to be willing to establish a relevant level of debate within the UN (or some other international
forum) to achieve agreement on it. At the moment, we are far
from this position. For the most part the developed countries,
as John Sewell so succinctly puts it, see their own problems as
essentially solvable by action among the rich countries themselves, with the existing international and financial institutions adequate to the task. The problems of the developing
countries are seen as primarily their own fault, and thus to be
solved on their own. International security is seen primarily
in military terms, and thus a matter of East-West relations, not
North-South.

The South sees this differently — but as yet, they have limited
power and insufficient unity in practice to utilise to the full
the power they have.

The East too sees this differently — but as yet, they have shown
little readiness to engage seriously in the construction and
negotiation of an effective international strategy.

Meanwhile, the world economy is in disarray, month by month it is nearer to deep recession and prolonged stagnation than at any time since the 1930s. The lessons of the post-war years — that national expansion within a frame of helpful and accommodating international institutions as occurred, for all their inadequacies, in much of the 1950s and 1960s — are forgotten or seem irrelevant. The primary task of the Third Development Decade should be to recreate a frame of effective international institutions and action to restore dynamism within the world economy. All the main country groupings of the world would have a share but special provision would be made for the poorer and weaker countries, so that they and especially the poorer sections of their populations benefit from accelerated development in the Decade ahead.

CHAPTER 2

The Third World's Views of the New International Development Strategy for the Third United Nations Development Decade

T. G. WEISS*

INTRODUCTION

The articulation of the International Development Strategy (IDS) for the Third United Nations Development Decade (DDIII) has come about for two reasons: successful efforts by developing countries to push their interests in the day-to-day work of international organizations; and the reluctant realisation by developed countries that their own fates could not be isolated completely from those of developing countries. The necessity to reorder global economic production and distribution patterns in order to improve the lot of the vast majority of poor citizens in developing countries — i.e. the content of what is generally known as the New International Economic Order (NIEO) — has virtually become the exclusive concern of international organizations.

A genuine shift in the principal concerns of international organizations and their staffs has occurred in recent years, a fact clearly illustrated by the importance attached to developmental issues. The debate of the Eleventh Special Session of

*The author is an Economic Affairs Officer at the United Nations Conference on Trade and Development (UNCTAD). The present article is the sole responsibility of its author and does not commit UNCTAD which does not necessarily endorse the opinions set forth. The author is grateful to Mr Bernard Chidzero, formerly Deputy Secretary-General of UNCTAD and presently Minister of Planning and Development in Zimbabwe, for his suggestions on the content and structure of the present article.

the General Assembly[1][†]or the publication of the findings of the
Brandt Commission[2]or the yearly overview by the World Bank[3]have
all received a great deal of attention from a multitude of
audiences and journals that would barely have been aware of the
existence of Third World concerns as little as a decade ago.

International organizations have traditionally been marginal not
only for so-called 'realist' scholars,[4]but for virtually all
citizens and national decision makers of developed countries,
with the exception of those directly connected with the study
or operation of international institutions. The reliability of
this generalization has gradually diminished during the last two
development decades. Decolonization led to a rapid expansion
of United Nations membership in the 1960s; and raw materials
prices and shortages during the 1970s helped developing countries
collectively to assert themselves as active members of the
international system in which they emphasized the work of the
United Nations more than did established, economically developed
states. Developing countries also articulated the life-and-
death importance of accelerating economic and social development
through the forum of the General Assembly; and they called for
the expansion of the financial and technical assistance programmes of existant international agencies, or the creation of
new agencies such as UNCTAD or UNIDO. The suggestion has also
been made to establish a 'Third World Secretariat' to counter-
vail the influence of OECD and other international organizations
such as the General Agreement on Tariffs and Trade (GATT), The
World Bank and the International Monetary Fund (IMF) perceived
as being dominated by developed countries. In any event, about
80 per cent of all United Nations resources and 90 per cent of
its personnel are at present devoted to improving human welfare
through economic and social development.[5]

Within this context, the present article examines the implications of the new International Development Strategy[6]as a plea
from the planet's have-nots[7]to participate more fully in the
benefits of economic growth during the coming ten years. The
present argument proceeds in four sections: (1) a description
of conditions presently circumscribing international debate;
(2) a discussion of the shortcomings of the previous IDS; (3)
an enumeration of the essential elements of the new IDS; and
(4) conclusions.

[†]The notes relating to the numerical superscripts appear at the
end of the chapter.

THE UNPROPITIOUS PRESENT

Preparations for the International Development Strategy could
not have been undertaken in less propitious circumstances. The
Third Development Decade opens under the most ominous conditions
that have menaced the Third World in recent memory. The results
of the preceding Development Decade and its accompanying strategy
have been highly disappointing; and the current global economic
situation is critical. The outlook for the world economy in
the decade which has just begun is far gloomier than it was at
the beginning of the 1970s.

Growth of the OECD economies hovered around 1 per cent in 1980
and will rise to only 2.7 per cent according to some forecasts
for 1981. Inflation in OECD countries averaged about 11 per
cent for 1980, probably falling only to 9.4 per cent in 1981.
At the same time balance of payments on current account for the
developed market economies showed a deficit of $50 billion in
1980, and will fall only slightly to $45 billion in 1981. These
figures partially explain why disbursements of official development assistance (ODA) remain less than half of the volume
targeted in the IDS for the Second Development Decade (DDII).

The volume of world exports grew by less than 3 per cent in 1980,
and is forecast to increase by 5 per cent in 1981. World export
prices are believed to have increased by 21 per cent in 1980,
and will increase by a further 9 per cent in 1981. As a result
of stagnant world trade and a sharp rise in the cost of manufactures, the terms of trade for primary commodities (excluding
petroleum) will probably continue to decline. Even with substantial borrowing permitting the non-oil exporting countries
to run deficits in the region of $70 billion in 1981, the vast
majority of developing countries will find it difficult to
achieve growth rates above 5 per cent.

Improvements in some of these trends are forecast by some for
the remainder of the decade. Without substantial structural
change, however, it is doubtful that the world economy will
overcome stagnation, high inflation and substantial balance-of-
payments problems. Nor are the results of the IDS for the last
Development Decade encouraging for the 1980s. On the basis of
data for the first eight years of the decade, certain conclusions
can be drawn.

The central objective of the last IDS, namely an average rate
of growth of 6 per cent per annum in GNP for developing countries,

was nearly achieved for these countries as a whole.[8] However,
this average rate of growth has been very unevenly distributed
and attained only as a result of the rapid progress achieved by
a small number of countries that were already relatively
developed or that enjoyed particularly favourable endowments of
natural resources, especially petroleum. Indeed, in the case
of the low-income countries, which account for half the total
population of the Third World excluding China, the average rate
of growth in the 1970s was little more than 3 per cent per year.
Because of population growth in these countries, the average rate
of increase in their *per capita* GNP was no more than about 1 per
cent. In fact, almost half of the thirty structurally weakest
countries, the so-called 'least developed', have actually registered negative rates of growth in income *per capita* during the
decade.

In short, a herculean effort is required of the international
community simply to prevent further deterioration. Observers
of international relations, in developed as well as developing
countries, are realising that the present crisis does not
represent a short-run disequilibrium. Longer-term structural
change is imperative and demands struggle and enlightened
adaptation. Amelioration of the present international economic
order will require an alternative global division of labour and
wealth. The recent period of stagnation and decline has unfortunately brought forth myopic, *ad hoc* and inward-looking
policy measures such as protectionism in the Western World
rather than those reflecting the fundamental disequilibrium of
the international economic system.

SHORTCOMINGS IN THE PREVIOUS INTERNATIONAL DEVELOPMENT STRATEGY

These depressing facts alone would suggest that, while some
targets have been attained, the IDS for DDII has been largely
a failure. It is in the poorest countries that an acceleration
of economic growth and an improvement of living conditions are
most urgent. Rather than dismissing the goals of the previous
Development Strategy as unviable, citizens of developed countries
committed to formulating an adequate response to the emergency
must analyze the reasons for failure. In particular, attention
must be focused on new constraints to development that have
emerged in recent years.[9]

What then were the shortcomings of the previous IDS? First,
official aid to developing countries did not increase according

to the proposed standard of 0.7 per cent per annum of the GNP
of developed countries. Although a number of Western countries
members of OECD's Development Assistance Committee (e.g. Sweden,
Denmark, Norway and the Netherlands) have attained or surpassed
this target, the actual average level is still only 0.3 per cent.
The percentages of the quantitatively most important donors —
the United States of America, the United Kingdom, the Federal
Republic of Germany and Japan — are not only far from the pre-
scribed target, but are, in fact, decreasing.

Second, and more important from the point of view of structural
change, the implementation of the last Development Strategy was
hampered by a series of crises that shook the world economy
during the latter part of the decade, preventing attainment of
the targets for trade expansion by developing countries. The
collapse of the Bretton Woods monetary system brought about the
depreciation of the dollar and the concomitant destabilisation
of exchange rates; petroleum shortages and the emergence of the
Organization of Petroleum Exporting Countries (OPEC) as an
important factor in determining oil prices provoked a steep and
continuing rise in the price of this essential commodity; and
general inflation and monetary instability led to the industrial
recession of 1974-1975, the deepest since the 1930s. By 1980
protectionism and chronic unemployment were rife, and the
present recession promises to be even more serious than the 1974-
1975 slowdown.

Nevertheless, the disappointments of the Second Development
Decade cannot be explained solely by these factors. The growth
achieved by the poorest developing countries was as unsatis-
factory during the early years of the decade, when economic
growth in the industrial countries was still relatively rapid,
as during the later crisis-ridden years of the decade. Since
UNCTAD's establishment in 1964 as an alternative to the General
Agreement on Tariffs and Trade (GATT),[10]the views of developing
countries have become more prominent. The principal theme of
the new International Development Strategy for the Eighties has
resulted: Something is fundamentally awry in the international
trade, monetary and financial systems; something is also wrong
with the operation of the market system in a world of unequal
partners; and there exist deep structural and international
defects and built-in obstacles to progress in the global economy.

The widespread demand for fundamental change, rather than simple
reform, developed gradually and crystallized in the mid 1970s.
Although the adoption of the text of the IDS for the Second
United Nations Development Decade[11]was a historical step in the

promotion of international co-operation, one must recall the
IDS's conceptual limitations. It was conceived to ameliorate
the widely accepted system of international relations.

A consensus emerged — first mainly among developing countries
but gradually in many developed countries as well — that a
radical alteration of the international economy was required in
order to improve the prospects of the vast majority of the
world's population. The emergence of this consensus at the
Sixth Special Session of the General Assembly resulted in the
mobilization of necessary support for the call to establish the
New International Economic Order.[12] This call for a thorough
overhauling of the international economic system in order to
make it more supportive of the development process was subsequently strengthened and made more precise in the Charter of
Economic Rights and Duties of States[13] and in the resolution on
development and international economic co-operation adopted by
the Seventh Special Session of the General Assembly.[14]

Although many developed countries fought to dilute these documents, they nonetheless reflect a fundamental change in the
prognosis for international development. The Third World's
development would never be a mere by-product of economic growth
in the industrial countries — even at the normal and expanding
rates of the 1960s, much less the stagnating ones of the late
1970s; and an adequate acceleration of their development could
not be brought about simply through a transfer of financial
resources, however large. To overcome the international
economy's structural disequilibrium the 'rules of the game' had
to be rewritten.

The NIEO is thus a blue-print for thorough-going change in the
existing mechanisms and institutional relations of the global
economic system that are inhibiting development and reinforcing
the developing countries' economic dependence. These mechanisms
and relations are those that govern the functioning of world
commodity markets, the marketing and distribution channels for
primary commodities, the international division of labour, the
unregulated activities of transnational corporations and international flows of trade, money, finance and technology. Developing countries are demanding effective sovereignty over their
own natural resources, stable and equitable prices for their
labour, a transformation of their economies and a weight equal
to their numbers in international decision-making processes.

In short, they are calling for a more equitable distribution of
the benefits of growth, whether publicly or privately generated.

Historically speaking, the General Assembly's special sessions
of 1974 and 1975 thus codified a new agreement about international economic woes.[15] The discussion in 1980 at the Eleventh
Special Session of the New International Development Strategy
for the Third United Nations Development Decade took place in
a fundamentally changed rhetorical framework within which the
new IDS was unquestionably to be directed towards the achievement of the objectives of the NIEO.

The need to base the new IDS on fundamental institutional and
structural change — rather than on mere appeals to developed
countries to increase their aid to and imports from developing
countries — is all the more obvious now that the economies of
the industrial countries are in a state of crisis. Developed
nations are increasingly resorting to protectionist measures of
the kind that have long discriminated against developing
countries and only exacerbate the effects of the present recession on feeble economies. Developing countries have been forced
either to cut back developmental expenditures or to increase
already enormous debts. At the same time the situation of the
masses of people in these countries remains unpalatable with
rampant hunger, disease, homelessness and unemployment.

THE MAIN OUTLINES OF THE NEW INTERNATIONAL DEVELOPMENT STRATEGY

What does the new IDS imply for citizens of the wealthy industrialized world? In an increasingly interdependent global
economy, the West's problems of stagflation and balance-of-
payments disequilibria cannot be solved without responding to
the demands of the NIEO. The acceleration of economic growth
in poor countries is vital for the growth of the world economy
and ultimately for world peace and stability. A meaningful
movement toward the establishment of the NIEO, and thereby a
more efficient and equitable international economic system will
require radical changes in the following areas: trade; money
and finance; economic co-operation among developing countries;
relations with the most disadvantaged countries; food; and
energy. Although 'reform' is a far more congenial concept to
the Western mind than 'revolution', the transformations in both
developed and developing countries propounded in the NIEO are
fundamental and represent an upheaval in long-established
expectations and behaviour patterns.

In the first place, the rules and principles governing international trade must be altered to restructure the international

division of labour in order to accommodate the growing industrial
potential and changing comparative advantage of developing
countries.[16] Revised rules and principles must reflect the concerns of developing countries in such issues as protectionism,
structural adjustment, preferential treatment for developing
countries, regulation of the activities of transnational corporations and elimination and control of restrictive business
practices. In this connexion, the negotiations now in progress
within the United Nations on a code of conduct for transnational
corporations and on restrictive business practices should be
completed speedily and successfully. Economic relations between
developing countries and the socialist countries must be re-
ordered to expand and diversify trade so that the benefits
presently accruing to the former are increased substantially.

The proposed restructuring of the international division of
labour is intended to apply not only to the industrial sector
but also to the primary commodity and services sectors. In the
case of primary commodities, the objective of transformation is
to provide a sound basis for industrialization. Early comple-
tion of negotiations under UNCTAD's auspices of the Integrated
Programme for Commodities, including the ratification of the
agreement for the establishment of the Common Fund, is therefore
a priority. The Integrated Programme and Common Fund seek not
only to stabilize prices of commodities, but also to facilitate
the expansion of commodity processing in developing countries
and the participation by these countries in the international
marketing and distribution of their own commodity exports.

Structural adjustments in developed countries necessarily
entail painful decisions and temporary dislocations of workers
and industries. However, adjustments that favour more imports
from developing countries, especially of manufactured products,
will generate greater purchasing power in developing countries
which in turn will create greater demand for capital goods and
other imports from developed countries. The net result will not
only be increased growth but also a more efficient international
division of labour and symmetrical division of benefits.

In spite of the recent loss of jobs and production in such industries as textiles and electronics, developed countries have
probably benefitted from trade-related industrial production far
more than developing countries both in terms of income and
employment. Concern over growth of the South's industrial base
appear strange when the North holds a large and increasing surplus in its trade with the South in manufacturers, a surplus

that amounted to no less than $105 billion in 1977. Calculations
for 1976 also indicate a net gain of approximately 1.5 million
jobs in the North from trade in manufacturers with developing
countries.[17]

The second principal area of structural change proposed by the
IDS for DDIII concerns the international monetary and financial
framework.[18] The overall objective is a substantial increase in
both private and public financial resources for developing
countries. These flows which have fluctuated wildly with political caprice, are to be set-up on predictable, continuous and
assured bases. More urgently, immediate measures are required
to deal with the grave balance-of-payments problems of many
developing countries resulting from increased energy prices and
other inflationary pressures which in 1980 alone provoked a
deficit of about $60 billion in these countries. Reform of the
financial framework should provide also for the establishment
of internationally agreed upon principles, procedures and
mechanisms for the future treatment of the debt.

Above all, the international monetary system must be modified
to ensure greater stability in exchange rates and greater international control over the creation and distribution of international liquidity. Serious consideration must be given to
links between the creation of liquidity and necessary resources
to finance developmental expenditures. Institutional reforms
should make it possible for developing countries to participate
effectively in the decision-making process of such bodies as
GATT, the World Bank and the IMF whose decision-making structures have long favoured the industrialized countries.

The third major field requiring vigorous action is economic co-
operation among developing countries.[19] The rhetoric of collective self-reliance must be translated into effective programmes.
While the main elements of such co-operation must be negotiated
by developing countries themselves, the international community
and all developed countries should endorse and support efforts
to strengthen this type of collaboration in accordance with
principles, guidelines and programmes already sketched by
developing countries in the "Arusha Programme of Collective
Self-Reliance" and the "Havana Guidelines on the Reinforcement
of the Collective Self-Reliance Among Developing Countries".[20]

While detailed programmes are yet to be elaborated, economic co-
operation among developing countries should be enhanced in the
areas of trade, money, finance, technology and transport with a
view toward accelerating the economic growth of developing

countries, reducing their external dependence and vulnerability, and strengthening their collective bargaining power and potential for autonomous growth.[21] Such programmes must also begin to specify measures for confronting the immense socio-economic problems and disparities of income distribution within develop-ing countries. While the new IDS skirts these issues, greater efforts must be made to redistribute the benefits of development among the vast majority of poor rather than mainly among elites.

A fourth principal recommendation of the new IDS is that, what-ever else occurs during the next Development Decade, much more significant efforts must be made on behalf of the poorest. Support is necessary for the special programme of measures for the least developed countries — the 31 economically weakest countries facing the most formidable structural problems.   In DDII, their annual average rate of growth was below 1 per cent, and 11 actually experienced negative growth rates. As a group they recorded declines in an agricultural production, manufac-turing output, gross domestic investment, export purchasing power and import volume. The new Development Strategy therefore strongly endorses the substantial new programme of action for the 1980s for the least developed countries, including the successful conclusion of the United Nations Conference on the Least Developed Countries in September 1981.[22]

In addition to these four major areas, the new IDS[23]focusses on two productive sectors so important as to call for special treatment; food[24]and energy.[25] More intensive efforts will be required substantially to increase food production in develop-ing countries while at the same time providing for adequate global food stocks.[26] Attention should also be given to elimin-ating protective measures by some developed countries that in-hibit the expansion of agricultural exports, production and processing by developing countries.

The IDS directs particular attention to energy problems in both North and South. Special attention, however, is given to the specific problems of developing countries in this area. Financial measures must be taken to recycle surpluses effectively and to meet the pressing balance-of-payments problems of develop-ing countries that import oil; and steps must also be taken to develop new sources of conventional forms of energy. To this end, more adequate financial and technical assistance should be provided to developing countries to expand energy exploration and exploitation, a proposal currently under active study by the World Bank. Unrestricted access by developing countries to the advanced energy technology of developed countries is also required. The Strategy also emphasizes the need to alter patterns of energy consumption and eventually to eliminate inefficient uses of hydrocarbons.

Since late 1973, citizens of developed countries have been staggering under continuous increases in the price of oil and are hence disinclined to consider with an open mind the point of view of developing countries on this crucial matter. Petroleum production and pricing is the sole area in which developing countries have demonstrated effective bargaining strength. One could argue that no negotiations on a new economic order, much less the establishment of a schedule in 1981 for global economic negotiations would have occurred without the appearance of OPEC and its solidarity with other developing countries in confrontations with the West. Acrimonious discussions about a timetable for global negotiations characterized the Eleventh Special Session, largely because of the recalcitrance of the United States, the United Kingdom and the Federal Republic of Germany. From the point of view of developing countries, energy problems cannot be separated from the broader context of development and of the need for institutional reforms in the fields of money, finance and trade.[27]

CONCLUSIONS

These are some key considerations of the new IDS in qualitative terms. In order to focus attention on the magnitude of change required in critical areas of policy, some quantitative targets, both overall and sectoral, have also been included. There was always great reluctance to set such targets in the past, in part because developed countries were hesitant to specify a barometer against which progress could be measured. Although the new IDS does not establish as many specific targets as a good number of participants had hoped, it proposes more than in the preceding IDS; and the specific figures could provide a basis for effective monitoring of progress in the Strategy's implementaion.[28]

Certain specific targets are higher than those set in the preceding decade (e.g. for developing countries, overall growth rates of 7 per cent and an average annual rate of growth in the manufacturing sector of 9 per cent); and others have been reaffirmed (the most important one being the aid target of 0.7 per cent of GNP in the developed countries to be increased to 1 per cent as soon as possible in the 1990s). Special emphasis has been placed on minimum growth targets for poor countries as well as for disadvantaged groups within all developing countries

(expressed in terms of infant mortality and life expectancy).
These latter targets are especially important if the deteriorating situation of the vast majority of the world's poor is not
to be overlooked in the well-known statistical problems pertain-
ing to averages. Rather than simply assuming that increases in
GDP are by definition a step forward, the new IDS recognises the
need to measure the actual benefits of growth in the lives of
poor people.

Particularly in the present inauspicious circumstances, the
International Development Strategy for the Third United Nations
Development Decade is extremely ambitious. Its realization is
the responsibility of all the planet's citizens, those in developed and in developing countries. Inhabitants of the wealthiest
countries of the world have a special responsibility to mobilize
support for policies that strengthen the groping efforts of
humanity to implement an improved international economic order.
Our response to the challenge of development in the eighties
must be not merely to agree on a body of rhetorical policies and
measures but to act decisively to implement them. In pursuing
this objective, political will — no less than enlightened self
interest — is of the essence.

NOTES

1 *Report of the Ad Hoc Committee of the Eleventh Special Session,*
   document A/S-11/25, 13 September 1980.

2 *North-South: A Programme for Survival,* the Report of the Independent Commission on International Development Issues
   under the Chairmanship of Willy Brandt (London, Pan Books,
   1980).

3 *World Development Report, 1980* (Washington, DC, The World
   Bank, August 1980.

4 For a discussion of the assumptions underlying conventional
   and alternative approaches to international politics see:
   Norman V. Walbek and Thomas G. Weiss, *A World Order Framework for Teaching International Politics* (New York, Institute
   for World Order Teaching Resources No 3, 1974).

5 See: Harold K. Jacobson, "The Changing United Nations", in
   Roger Hilsman and Robert C. Good, (eds.), *Foreign Policy in
   the Sixties: The Issues and the Instruments* (Baltimore Johns
   Hopkins, 1965), pp. 67-89; and *Networks of Interdependence*

(New York, Knopf, 1979), pp. 21-144. For a thorough and readable general study of the economic and social programmes of the UN system, see: Mahdi Elmandjra, *The United Nations System: An Analysis* (Hamden, CT, Archon Books, 1973). A partial explanation for ignorance about the importance of welfare programming and for the relative concentration on the UN's image as a feeble guarantor of security, particularly in the Western world, is the poor coverage given to international economic and social activities by the mass media. See: Alexander Szalai, with Margaret Croke and Associates, *The United Nations and the News Media* (New York, Unitar Books, 1972).

It is important at the outset to specify that a dichotomous view of political and social issues is not appropriate. Interdependencies exist between the political and socio-economic realms of international co-operation. During the early years of the UN, there was a tendency to draw a sharp line between the political aspects of maintaining peace ('high politics') that were in the competence of the United Nations itself, and the technical or nonpolitical functions ('low politics') of specialized agencies. During the 1960s this difference was reduced and became more subtle as technical efforts came to be seen as 'peace building', and as an indispensable complement to the more political 'peace maintenance'. In the 1970s the trend was more toward a global perspective and interdependencies in which few economic or social issues did not involve the crucial issues of high politics. Hence, there is increasingly less of a demarcation between the economic, social, and cultural spheres, and the political and military aspects of international peace. For analytical purposes, it is nonetheless useful to discuss separately these two sets of problems.

6   The text of the *International Development Strategy for the Third United Nations Development Decade* is found in document A/35/464, 23 October 1980. Subsequent footnotes will include only "IDS, Section I" (Preamble), "IDS, Section II" (Goals and objectives), "IDS, Section III" (Policy measures) and "IDS, Section IV" (Review and appraisal of the implementation of the new International Development Strategy).

7   The author is not presuming to speak on behalf of the poor, but he does believe that his position within the UNCTAD secretariat, the widely-recognized lobbying group of the Third World in international organizations, does afford a

sound vantage point for observing the evolution of development issues. As a native of a wealthy country speaking to
other citizens of developed countries, he wishes to interpret
the importance of the IDS for his fellows in the North. For
the most recent official articulation of the UNCTAD
secretariat's views see: *Preparation of a Draft for the Contribution of UNCTAD to the Formulation of the International
Development Strategy for the Third United Nations Development
Decade*, note by the UNCTAD secretariat, document TD/B/AC.31/2,
15 January 1980.

8   See particularly the preceding discussion by Richard Jolly
    in which he clearly indicates that both DDI and DDII ought
    to be given high marks according to the straightforward test
    of achievement. For a thorough historical analysis of the
    first two development decades, see: Colin Legum, *et al.*,
    The First UN Development Decade and its lessons for the 1970s
    (New York, Praeger, 1970); and The Committee for Development
    Planning, "Report on 16th Session", document E/1980/3,
    Supplement 2, January 1980.

9   In this regard, it would be misleading to imply — as is often
    the case in the rhetoric of international fora and their
    accompanying resolutions — that only external impositions
    and constraints have forced developing countries into the
    present economic quagmire. All too frequently there has
    been a clear refusal to face squarely a host of largely in-
    ternal problems, be they questions of tribal or ethnic
    rivalries or faulty economic policies. However, it is
    equally clear that the 'rules of the game' applying to the
    international economy clearly favour the 'have's' over the
    'have-nots'. As the IDS is essentially an attempt to codify
    alternative operating procedures for inter-state behaviour,
    with only passing reference made to obvious internal problems,
    the present article will concentrate upon the former.

10 For a discussion of the politics surrounding UNCTAD's foun-
    dation as an alternative to the rich man's sanctuary of GATT,
    see: Branislov Gosivic, *UNCTAD: Compromise and Conflict*
    (Leiden, A. W. Sijthoff, 1972), *passim*; Diego Cordovez,
    *UNCTAD and Development Diplomacy: From Confrontation to
    Strategy* (London, Journal of World Trade Law, 1970),
    especially Chapter III, "The UNCTAD-GATT Relationship," pp.
    57-72; Kamal Hagras, *United Nations Conference on Trade and
    Development: A Case Study in UN Diplomacy* (New York, Praeger,
    1965), *passim*; and R. L. Rothstein, *Global Bargaining: UNCTAD*

and the Quest for a New International Economic Order
(Princeton, Princeton Univ Press, 1979).

11 General Assembly Resolution 2626(XXV), 24 October 1970.

12 See: "Declaration on the Establishment of a New International
    Economic Order", General Assembly Resolution 3201(S-VI) and
    "Programme of Action on the Establishment of a New Inter-
    national Economic Order", General Assembly Resolution 3202
    (S-VI), 1 May 1974.

13 General Assembly Resolution 3281(XXIX), 12 December 1974.

14 General Assembly Resolution 3362(S-VII), 16 September 1975.

15 In relationship to the changing role of the United Nations,
    one should note that the first five special sessions of the
    General Assembly were concerned with international conflicts
    and the United Nations' role in maintaining peace. Four of
    the last six special sessions, including all of the most
    politicised ones, as well as the host of *ad hoc* global con-
    ferences on such issues as environment, population, food,
    energy, etc., have all dealt exclusively with development
    issues.

16 See: "IDS, Section III", part A.

17 See: Geoffrey Renshaw, *Employment, Trade and North-South Co-
    operation* (Geneva, International Labour Organization, 1980).

18 See: "IDS, Section III", part E.

19 See: "IDS, Section III", part J.

20 See: documents TD/236 and A/34/542.

21 It should be noted that many observers had hoped that the
    IDS would make references to specific projects in regions
    including several developing countries. In this fashion a
    concrete commitment could have been elicited from developed
    countries to action directly linked to facilitating collab-
    oration among developing countries. The new IDS, however,
    makes only a cursory reference to general documents such as
    The Lagos Plan of Action for the Implementation of the Mon-
    rovia Strategy for the Economic Development of Africa (see
    document A/S-11/14, annex I) and The Transport Decade for

Africa (see document E/CN.14/726) that themselves are ex-
cessively general or have no workable listing of priorities.

22 The degree of international consensus on this problem is
    greater than in any other. In fact, one of only two sub-
    stantive resolutions at the Eleventh Special Session of the
    General Assembly concerned the poorest countries. See:
    *Measures to meet the critical situation in the least developed
    countries*, document A/S-11/AC.1/L.7, 13 September 1980.

23 The author has not dealt with a host of other issues that
    were judged of less analytical importance than those included
    above. For example, the new IDS also prescribes measures
    and policies for dealing with a number of other specific
    problems facing developing countries. These include the
    rapid technological transformation of the economies of these
    countries, their effective participation in such services as
    communications, transport (in particular shipping) and in-
    surance. Furthermore, the strategy also addresses itself
    to the special problems faced by geographically disadvantaged
    countries (land-locked and islands).

24 See: "IDS, Section III", part C.

25 See: "IDS, Section III", part H.

26 The interested reader should consult: *Report of the World
    Conference on Agrarian Reform and Rural Development, Rome,
    12-20 July 1979* (WCARRD/REP), document A/34/485; the *Report
    of the Intergovernmental Group on Grains of the Food and
    Agriculture Organization of the United Nations (FAO) on world
    food security*, document CCP: GR.75/9, August 1975; and the
    *Report of the FAO Committee on World Food Security on its
    fifth session*, document CL.78/10.

27 For the text of the timetable on global negotiations which
    met with the approval of all countries except these three,
    see: *Procedures and time-frame for the global negotiations*,
    document A/S-11/AC.1/L.1/Rev. 12 September 1980.

28 As in the previous decade, a series of review and appraisal
    exercises will occur at the sectoral, regional and global
    levels in order to monitor the implementation of the new IDS.
    In contrast with the previous text, however, the IDS for the
    Third Development Decade actually specifies that a general
    review will be conducted by the General Assembly in 1984 and
    that sectoral and regional reviews are to be envisaged. See:
    "IDS, Section IV".

CHAPTER 3

EC Policy and the Third Development Decade

KLAUS VON HELLSDORFF

"For Europeans the question of North-South relations is of major importance. Our needs and our deficiencies require close co-operation with the Third World, and the promotion of a continuing relationship with the people of the South, who want to develop, and who will do so. For the Community this is a moral duty, a political imperative, and a vital economic necessity." This statement of Claude Cheysson, then the Commissioner for Development of the European Community (EC), made in 1977 is now more accurate than ever. If it is mainly for the Church to re-call the moral duty, and for governments to act on political imperatives, the Community's function is to propose to the governments of it's member states' common activities in keeping with its common economic imperatives and to implement them to the limit that agreements amongst them have been reached.

In the field of North-South relations, remarkable achievements have been made, particularly since — and to a large extent because — the United Kingdom joined the Community. The first 'oil shock' a few months later was another important element. At the end of the eighties and of the Second Development Decade, EC, as such, and in addition to continuing important bi-lateral co-operation efforts of it's member states, has established a unique network of co-operation agreements with nearly three quarters of the developing countries. Concluded for at least five years or even an unlimited period, all of these agreements reflect the common concern for stability and security in an essential area of international economic relations: trade. They are based on the principle of equality with full respect for each side's political and cultural identity, in spite of significant differences in economic production. They also provide, in general, institutionalised mechanisms for consultation on all matters of mutual interest. Most of them — in particular the

47

Lomé Convention which was recently renewed for 5 years (1981-1985) — include substantial financial assistance and a set of measures to meet the specific development needs of the 60 African, Caribbean and Pacific (ACP) countries, who have signed it (Zimbabwe being the latest).

In addition, generalised tariff preferences for all developing countries (including China and Romania); substantial food aid, worth some EUA300 billion and modest though steadily increasing financial assistance, both direct and through non-governmental organizations, for the least developed countries are granted on an annual basis. Unfortunately, natural catastrophes as well as armed conflicts have made emergency relief a rapidly growing imperative in the last years. Thus development aid has become by now the second most important item in EC's budget after the Common Agricultural Policy.

The Community's specific contribution to the world development effort lies less in the amount of resource transfers — these represent only between 10 per cent and 15 per cent of the total flows of official development aid granted by its member states — than in the comprehensive way it has tried to establish long-standing, stable relations, based on mutual respect and interest with a large number of developing countries.

If I add that the Community is the major importer (30 per cent) from, and exporter (40 per cent) to, all developing countries with the lowest (if any) custom's tariffs and that it's members supply 40 per cent of total (world) official development assistance, (0.48 per cent of GNP in 1979), one might be mislead to believe that Europe is doing enough.

Far from it, especially in the context of continuing need by the Third World, as the Brandt Report has dramatically demonstrated. Furthermore, it is essential to note that the EC (also member states bilateral aid included) favours one region of the Third World: Africa. More should be done in the others. When the first Lomé Convention was signed in 1975, both sides felt they had established 'a pioneering model of co-operation between poor and rich countries'. Yet five years later we are aware that this model has not been replicated either by EC with other countries or by other industrialised countries.

The facts also indicate that we cannot afford to ignore the legitimate aspirations of the vast majority of mankind living in the South, for it will by necessity affect our own living standard and way of life.

Thus, although the EC still takes the lead among rich countries,
including OPEC, much more has to be done in order to prestall
the dramatic problems of the world economy in recession. Under
the significant heading "If we stopped to pretend that nothing
has changed in the economic order", Claude Cheysson recently
stated: "From full employment in the early seventies we have
passed today to 7 million unemployed in the Community; 40 per
cent of them are less than 25 years old.... Is this the same
world? In the same period the oil price passed from 3 dollars
to 32.36 dollars.... Is this the same world? In 1970 the Third
World represented about ¼ of the Community's exports, the United
States 16 per cent. In 1979 the same Third World represents 40
per cent of our exports and the US have gone down to 12 per cent.
One billion dollars of steel exports to the Third World means
25000 full-time employments in the Community."

It is thus no surprise that the Community has taken an active
interest in the definition of the framework for the next ten
or more years of development efforts of the Third World countries
and the action the international community will have to take to
support those efforts (Strategy for the Third Development Decade),
and also in the resumption of the global North-South Dialogue.

The essential collective interests which must be urgently dealt
with have been defined by the Community as follows:

(1) Countering the threat of deep and widespread recession
     facing the economies of both North and South: There are
     clear risks to the international economic system and world
     peace itself in current developments; these risks could
     become aggravated with the strangulation of the poorest
     developing countries and cessation of the growth process
     in middle-income developing countries.

(2) Easing world hunger: Insecurity of food supplies at world
     level is beyond doubt the least tolerable of all forms of
     uncertainty, and it is an absolute moral imperative for the
     international community to reduce this insecurity.

(3) Organizing the transition to a less oil-dependent world
     economy: The foreseeable imbalance between the oil supplies
     and potential demand over the next few years places a
     serious question mark over the chances of accelerating the
     growth and development processes. The second 'oil crisis'
     and the continuing tremors it has set up show that dis-
     orderly escalation of oil prices and uncertainties of
     supply will remain a problem until some way is found of

establishing comprehensive co-operation between energy
producers and consumers.

No single country or group of countries — not even the Community —
has the means to attain to even one of these objectives. The
prospects of effective global North-South negotiations are still
uncertain. The considerations on 'North-South Dialogue — search
for security and prevision' submitted to the European Council in
December 1980 are an effective way of learning about the crucial
issues for the policy of the European Community in the 1980s.
1980s.

THE NORTH-SOUTH DIALOGUE: THE SEARCH FOR
SECURITY AND PREDICTABILITY[1]

In 1981 the North-South talks will play a major part in international relations. Will this be the year when a real dialogue
gets under way between all the industrialized countries and all
the developing countries, including the OPEC members, or will
the deepening recession and the steady deterioration of the
climate of international relations result in confusion and confrontation?

In any event the timetable will be a tight one both in the UN
and the specialized agencies,[2] and in the more narrowly-based
talks between Europe and other regions.

The opportunities provided by this schedule — or created as the
occasion offers — should make it possible to tackle seriously
some of the issues most vital to the future development of
economic relations between the countries of North and South.
They offer scope for progress in the search for greater security
and predictability in relations among all the parties.

SECURITY AND PREDICTABILITY: LEITMOTIV
OF THE GLOBAL NEGOTIATIONS

In this connexion it is clearly important that the global negotiations in New York get off the ground. Firstly, because this

---

[1]Communication from the Commission of the European Communities
to the European Council, Luxembourg, 1-2 December 1980.

[2]See Appendix for timetable.

would help restore a climate of confidence, currently seriously
compromised on both sides; secondly, and above all, because it
has now emerged that this search for security and predictability
is to some extent the common denominator of all the parties'
negotiating objectives: this is true in the fields of recycling
and development financing and of commodities, in energy and food
security, in access to markets and the value of surplus countries'
financial assets.

This gives the measure of the complexity of the North-South
Dialogue, which the global negotiations are intended to intensify
and advance. They will not be able to advance, they will indeed
be meaningless, unless the main protagonists on the world stage
all feel truly concerned. This means that all the major issues
must be tackled in relation with each other: this is essential
and can be undertaken while still observing the jurisdiction
and functions of the various specialized decision-making bodies.

The Community, one of whose constant objectives during the
preparations for the global negotiations has been to involve
both the major industrialized countries and the oil producers
in the search for mutually beneficial solutions to the major
economic problems afflicting the world economy, will therefore
have to work hard to win both sides over to a balanced and
attractive agenda and to procedural rules acceptable to everyone.

Already, without waiting for the actual opening of the global
negotiations, and indeed even assuming that it will be delayed,
the Community should be working out its positions for the resumption of a dialogue between North and South which in any
event cannot be confined to the UN forum.

THE DEVELOPMENT OF A COMMUNITY APPROACH IN
THE NORTH-SOUTH DIALOGUE

The Community, its Member States and industries have an obvious
interest in seeing the gradual formulation of rules to ensure
greater security and predictability in North-South relations in
all spheres; on this depend the terms on which we get our
supplies, and access to markets whose rapid expansions has been
one of the few growth factors for many sectors of our economies
over the last few years, and must become so again as soon as
possible. In order to play an active part in the negotiations,
the Community must speak with one voice. Since the Paris Conference in 1977, experience has shown that the North-South

Dialogue only moves forward when the Community presents a united
front and gives a lead, the most recent example being the negotiations for the cocoa agreement.

But it must also help demonstrate the scope for progress at
world level both in the other North-South forums and by its own
actions. At the multilateral level the role which the Community
must play is to initiate and give an impetus, as a matter of
priority, to:

(1) The negotiation of the commodity agreements scheduled for
    the end of 1980 and for 1981 and the implementation of the
    agreements concluded recently.

(2) The work being done within the Bretton Woods institutions
    to increase rapidly the facilities they can offer the
    developing countries and to diversify their methods of
    operation in order to be able to respond effectively to the
    problems facing those countries because of the considerable
    worsening of their external deficits. To this end, a number
    of initiatives were recently taken by the Fund and the Bank,
    in particular on the setting up of an energy subsidiary.[3]

At the level of direct action by the Community via its own
measures:

(1) The participation of Community mechanisms in recycling
    must complement action by the international financial
    organizations (notably by means of co-financing operations
    shared jointly by the Community and the Arab funds).

(2) With regard to official development assistance, our most
    characteristic form of action in favour of the least
    developed countries is embodied in the relations governed
    by the Lomé Convention, whose exemplary value must there-
    fore be increased, particularly in the development of rural
    communities.

(3) Our contribution to food security must be improved in
    accordance with some of the guidelines laid down by the
    European Parliament after the debate on world hunger and
    recently endorsed by the Council.

---

[3]It should be noted that these initiatives have been held in
abeyance, pending in particular settlement of the question of
observer status for the PLO.

(4) In view of its responsibilities with regard to trade the
     community, which supports the development of a system of
     free trade, must make progress on the Generalized System
     of Preferences and renewal of the Multifibre Arrangement.
     It must increase the opportunities for consultations with
     its Southern partners in order to anticipate developments
     expected on both sides.

(5) Strengthening of the European Monetary System will enable
     the Community to play a bigger role in recycling capital,
     to play a more effective part in the effort required to
     strengthen the international monetary system and to respond
     to some of the principal problems facing the developing
     countries.

CLOSER RELATIONS BETWEEN THE COMMUNITY AND ITS NORTH-SOUTH PARTNERS

The Community's scope for action within the North-South Dialogue
is also to a very large extent linked to the development of our
direct relations with the United States, which often has a
different approach to North-South problems, which makes Community
cohesion more difficult to achieve. It is therefore essential
at the present time that the Community position be explained to
the United States via increased contacts at all levels (Congress,
the Executive, public opinion) to promote awareness of the importance to Europe of the North-South dimension and reduce
possible divergences of analysis. In this connection industrialized countries could play a useful role in strengthening Western
cohesion: the Community must therefore seize every opportunity
to compare its views on North-South relations with those of
Canada, Japan and the Scandinavian countries.

Also, global negotiations may help to get the necessary discussions going with the oil countries but they will not be
enough in themselves. Direct relations will have to be established by the Community in order to deal with matters which are
of interest to these countries to varying degrees. This category covers firstly all questions linked with the security and
real value of the financial assets accumulated by some countries
surplus to their development capacity. Secondly, it refers to
the search for security and predictability in the supply of
development inputs for those countries which have the capacity
to develop, namely the adequate reliability of suppliers of
certain consumer goods (mainly foodstuffs), the encouragement
of joint ventures with our companies, and the prospect of access
to our own market for processed products.

Lastly, because the political dimension must be constantly present, 'summits' of all kinds — whether they be between Northern
countries, Southern countries, or North and South — must discuss
these issues without, however, taking over from the competent
international bodies.

THE INTERNAL POLITICAL DIMENSION
OF THE NORTH-SOUTH DIALOGUE

The result of all this is that progress in North-South relations
will take place in many forums and at various levels; all these
sets of negotiations are complementary and interdependent. There
is, however, also a mutual dependence between progress at international (or inter-regional) level and the domestic situation in
each of our countries:

(i)   Our economies will benefit from selling more goods on
      better terms and from having secure terms for their
      supplies. The development of our partners has spin-offs
      for us which must be foreseen more clearly, discussed with
      them and included among our criteria for restructuring.
      This will mean involving the economic and social forces
      in each of our countries and at Community level.

(ii) The mobilization of public opinion is therefore crucial.
      The public must be made more aware of interdependence and
      its direct repercussions on the level of employment. There
      must be more discussion in parliaments, trade unions, non-
      governmental associations and at regional level, and the
      media must be used.

APPENDIX: NORTH-SOUTH TIMETABLE FOR 1981

(i)   *Global:* opening of the global negotiations on inter-
       national economic co-operation plus a number of restric-
       ted meetings of Heads of State or Government from North
       and South.

(ii)   *Monetary and financial:* implementation of the guidelines
       adopted by the IMF's Interim Committee and Managing
       Director, increase in the resources of the World Bank
       Group (and setting up of an 'energy' subsidiary in
       accordance with Mr McNamara's proposals).

(iii) *Food security:* wheat agreement, new food aid convention, security stockbuilding, replenishment of IFAD, etc.

(iv) *Trade:* renegotiation of the Multifibre Arrangement, GATT
      and UNCTAD talks on trade policy and restructuring
      measures.

 (v) *Commodities:* agreements to be concluded on cocoa, tin,
      jute and implementation of the agreement on the Common
      Fund.

(vi) *Aid to the poorest:* conference on the least developed
      countries.

CHAPTER 4

British Government Policy and the Third Development Decade

Government Policy in the Eighties

NEIL MARTEN

I am grateful to have been invited to contribute to this volume
on the important subject of the challenge of development in the
80s.

Two events in particular in 1980 have focused world attention
on the vital issue of international development. The first was
the publication in February of that year of the report of the
Brandt Commission. This important report, with its unanimous
findings by the 18 distinguished persons who made up the Commission, represented a valuable contribution to our understanding
of many of the issues involved. The second event was the
Special Session of the United Nations General Assembly which met
in the summer. This, too, rightly concentrated on the same
topic.

Underlying both of these was the stark reality of the aggravated
world economic situation, in which the Western industrialised
countries faced deepening economic difficulties; and the developing countries which, with a few notable exceptions, experienced
a worsening of their present economic situation and prospects
for the future. Against this background I regard it as a major —
and underpublicised — achievement for consensus to have been
reached on the international development strategy for the decade
ahead and the years beyond that.

The main theme of the Brandt report is the interdependence of
all countries in the world economy. This was also recognised
at the Special Session, and my Government seeks to emphasise
the concept. It is a concern which has influenced the policy
(of successive British Governments, as well as other Western
Governments) of helping to promote economic development in the
Third World.

There is real concern about the prospects of developing countries, especially the poorest. It is said that over 800 million people in the world today live in absolute poverty. It is these millions of people, who make up one fifth of the total world population, who are most at risk. They are constantly exposed to hunger, disease and homelessness. Further, the threat of natural disasters and various forms of unrest — tribal warfare, civil war, border disputes — frequently are added to their already precarious situation. These problems are compounded by the frightening increase in the world population. By the end of the century it is said that there could be two billion more mouths to feed.

This prospect alone calls for real and urgent efforts to be made to improve food production and its distribution to those most in need; and also to promote population planning. Otherwise the grim alternative is that the prospects of the poorest countries will become even bleaker. Prospects for the developing countries without oil have been worsened by slower growth in the industrial countries (on whom they depend for their export markets) and by rising debt. Increased oil prices and general inflationary pressures carry major responsibility for these trends. The prospects for the poorest developing countries are more bleak because they are less able to borrow to maintain their past economic progress.

These difficulties threaten to cancel out the progress which many of them have, with great effort and determination, achieved over the last 30 years. This is another aspect of their plight which commands urgent attention. The latest World Bank report points out that, in the absence of renewed growth, "hundreds of millions of very poor people will live and die with little or no improvement in their lot".

This once again brings us back to the factor of interdependence. Renewed growth as called for by the World Bank will not only directly benefit the poorer countries. It will also benefit the industrialised countries. All countries must work together to fight against poverty, in their own interest as much as that of other countries. It has become customary to see the world as divided into a rich North and a poor South. Indeed, this is the normal framework in which the greater part of negotiations on international economic questions takes place. On one side there are the so-called 'Group of 77', the developing countries. On the other there are the developed countries which are members of the Organization for Economic Co-operation and Development (OECD).

However, although this is the customary framework for negotiations, it is altogether inadequate and indeed misleading.
It suggests a community of economic interests amongst the
developing countries which in reality does not exist. Some members of the 77 become major producers and exporters of industrial
goods, and significant recipients of the major part of foreign
investment in developing countries.

Others, the majority, are faced with a continued battle for
economic survival, with a major part of their population sub-
sisting on the very fringes of existence. These countries have
been unable for the most part to attract foreign private investment or financial flows, and are likely to be dependent on inflows of concessional assistance for a very long time.

Then there are the oil producers, most of whom have seen their
foreign exchange surpluses grow to quite extraordinary levels,
particularly since the 1979 oil price increases. It is self-
evident that they must assume responsibility for recycling a
greater share of their surpluses, particularly by the provision
of greater flows of concessional assistance for the benefit of
the countries most in need. Despite their surplus wealth, OPEC
flows of official assistance amounted to less than a quarter of
those from the OECD countries in 1979.

Nor are these major groupings the end. Within each of them
there are wide divergences between individual countries: as,
indeed, there are within the countries of the OECD. The reason
for emphasising this diversity is not to make a debating point.
It is to indicate that, if progress is to be made in tackling
the vital problems of world development, it is not satisfactory
to assume that there are basically two economic groupings — one
of the North, and the other of the South. We must start from an
altogether more sophisticated understanding of the complex
economic realities.

Nor is that all. The division between North and South too often
ignores the countries of the Soviet Bloc. They are significant
enough on the world stage, and yet the contribution of the
Soviet Union and its wealthier Eastern European allies to the
two preceding development decades has been totally inadequate.
They could offer substantially increased trading opportunities
to the Third World. They could provide much more in the form
of official assistance and contribute to the various multilateral
institutions. It is essential that they do so henceforth.

Having described the setting as we see it, I shall now briefly set out the Government's policies in the main areas of concern for the forthcoming decade.

The most important contribution which Britain can make towards the objective of a more prosperous world is to restore a buoyant rate of growth in its own economy, as indeed must all the industrialised countries. For this it is vital for inflation first to be brought under control. A country which is dogged by inflation cannot play its proper role in the world economy.

Persistent inflation will reduce the capacity of the developed countries to help the developing world through aid, trade and investment. That is why the fight against inflation is, and must remain, the first priority for Britain and the other industrialised countries which are facing it. Once this has been won, then this will be a major first step on the road towards restoring the health of the world economy.

Despite the fact that the fight against inflation is not yet won, Britain is nevertheless continuing to make a major contribution towards the development of the Third World in a variety of ways, and certainly intends to do so throughout the decade. One of the most significant ways of doing this is through the encouragement of private flows in development. Private financial flows already provide the bulk of the needs for external finance of the middle-income developing countries. The financial markets will continue to be of major importance in recycling the surplus revenues which have accrued to the oil producing countries.

There is a central role here for the British institutions in the City of London. The policy of the Government is to facilitate both financial flows and private direct investment. Private investment also brings great benefits to developing countries in terms of technology, training and management expertise.

Britain has eliminated exchange controls, thus freeing the flow to developing countries of both finance and investment. The Government has ensured that the tax structure does not obstruct companies wishing to invest abroad. Similarly we have entered into double taxation agreements with a number of countries which are generous and help to promote private capital flows. The developing countries themselves have an important part to play in this process. They will be more successful in encouraging such investment if the conditions, both political and economic, which it is within their own control to influence, are made as welcoming as possible.

Equally important to the developing world is the stimulation of trade, through which the poorer countries can promote their own development. It is encouraging that, despite the economic dif- ficulties world-wide, both at the GATT multilateral trade nego- tiations which were successfully concluded in 1979 and at the fifth conference of the UNCTAD in Manila it was clear that both developing and developed countries were aware that protectionism was no answer to world recession.

The European Community has continued to adopt an increasingly liberal attitude to imports from developing countries. A recent example of this is the agreement reached on jute with India and Bangladesh, under which existing quotas will be progressively relaxed over the next few years — leading to complete liberaliza- tion thereafter. The Community is also reviewing its general- ised scheme of preferences, with the aim of simplifying the scheme and directing more of its benefits to the poorer develop- ing countries.

We would like to see an increasing emphasis on relieving the plight of the poorest and least competitive developing countries. As a trading nation ourselves, I like to think that we are more sensitive than most to the problems of the developing countries who are similarly dependent on international trade. Witness for example the IMPO/EXPO developing country trade fair mounted in London in 1979, and other British contributions to the trade promotion efforts of the less developed countries. These have been organized both bilaterally through the United Kingdom Trade Agency and internationally through the European Community and the International Trade Centre UNCTAD/GATT in Geneva.

Britain, too, can benefit from such policies. By helping the Third World to become less poor and more creditworthy, we both protect existing overseas markets for Britain and develop new ones for our goods and services. Trade is essentially a two way process, and those who still see assistance in the field of trade as charity are taking a very shortsighted view.

While a liberal international trading regime is of vital import- ance, it remains the case, as I said earlier, that most of the developing countries, and certainly the poorest, will remain largely dependent on a substantial inflow of concessionary assistance — both on a government-to-government basis and through the multilateral agencies — if they are to sustain any- thing like an acceptable rate of economic growth. Britain's contribution to this process remains substantial, even though reductions in planned aid expenditures have had to be made as

part of the Government's efforts as a whole to bring inflation
under control. This is a matter of regret, and we hope that
when the British economy is again restored to health our aid
will once again increase.

The constraints that exist on the provision of official concessionary assistance make it all the more important for this
scarce resource to be distributed where it is most needed, and
used as effectively as possible. The emphasis has to be on the
poorest countries: some two thirds of Britain's bilateral assistance is allocated in this way, and of our substantial contributions to the multilateral development institutions a very
high proportion goes to those most in need. I believe it right
that this emphasis on the poorest should continue.

At the same time I believe that the forms of aid should be
appropriate for the needs of the recipient countries, and that
the quality should be enhanced by the terms on which it is given.
I take some pride in the fact that our terms of aid are among
the most generous offered by donor countries, and that we continue to be a major source of technical advice for developing
countries — both directly and through the multilateral agencies —
in the provision of experts, consultants and training. The
development of human skills is a keystone of advancement, and
technical co-operation between donor and recipient is thus of
central importance — a fact long recognised in the British aid
programme.

Beyond that, I am sure that there is little dispute over the
areas of emphasis in which developed and developing countries
have to co-operate. The problems of food production and distribution, and of the need to exploit new sources of energy, have
long been recognised: but they remain critical. The developing
countries themselves have much to do in ensuring conditions
that facilitate development in these key sectors, but we too
must be ready to contribute, as we have over the years, because
effective collaboration in these sectors will bring benefits to
us all.

An Alternative Conservative View and Response

STEPHEN DORRELL

If for no other reason than that I am a very young member of
parliament, I cannot claim to be speaking on behalf of the
Government. That is perhaps both a strength and a weakness, but

it is quite clearly the truth. While I shall be making some
statements about the government's official attitude towards
development assistance, I would prefer to concentrate on a back-
bencher's view of precisely where our aid and development policy
is or should be going in four areas:

(1)   official development aid;

(2)   trade policy;

(3)   private investment;

(4)   the broader spectrum against which governmental decisions
      are being taken, during what the United Nations has desig-
      nated the 'Third Development Decade'.

The Government's views on its aid policy could be summarized in
the following manner. It is correct for Britain to have a substantial aid policy; and it is in our interests, both politically
and commercially, to promote economic and social development in
developing countries. Aid helps to reduce global poverty and
contributes to the growth of world trade. Our ability to support
an aid programme from public funds is dependent on the state of
our economy, and this must be the government's overriding
priority. In deploying our official aid resources, due regard
shall continue to be made for the developmental objectives of
the receiving country which aid can serve, but we shall also
seek to ensure that aid is fully supportive also of the United
Kingdom's interests. Relief of world poverty is a proper aim of
the international community, since it helps to create conditions
for greater peace and stability and contributes to the growth
of trade. It is in our national interests to do what we can
through the official aid programme to help the development process. Expenditure on Britain's official development programme
in the current financial year is expected to total a gross
figure of £840 million.

The Government's overriding aim is to restore Britain's economy,
and it is thus essential to reduce the share of resources taken
by public expenditure. We recognise the value of the contribution which overseas aid can make to the development of the
poorer countries of the world; but when considering where reductions in public expenditure can be made, it is not possible
to exempt this programme. Overseas aid will have to bear a
share of the cuts which the conservative Government has decided
to make. Nevertheless, our aid programme will remain a substantial one, and we shall continue to apply the funds available
to the greatest possible effect.

Some facts and figures about British aid indicate that our
programme compares well with those of other developed countries.
Britain's net official development assistance for 1978 amounted
to 0.48 per cent of GNP. The 1978 average was 0.35 per cent for
all the other donor countries who are members of the Development
Assistance Committee (DAC). Including private flows, the UK had
a *per capita* flow to the developing world running at 3.35 per
cent of GNP. In evaluating UK performance two points should be
kept in mind. First, the Pearson Commission's 0.7 per cent
target for aid was in fact part of a total target of 1 per cent
of GNP for flows to the developing world with an additional 0.3
per cent to have been made up by private flows. While British
Governments of both political parties have always accepted the
1 per cent overall target, the 0.7 per cent has never been
accepted by either political party in this country as the aim
of official development assistance. I suppose that anyone in
this country is entitled to say that as compared with the 1 per
cent target for total flows set out by Pearson, the 3.35 per
cent that we achieved in 1978 is not actually a bad result.

However, one must acknowledge that the total allocation represents a 14 per cent reduction, in real terms, of foreign
assistance in the present fiscal year. While the Government
clearly believes that overseas aid had to be part of overall
expenditure cuts, such reductions are, in my view, to be much
regretted, particularly when simultaneous increases in defense
expenditures are justified.

Further, there are policy changes that could compensate for aid
and other expenditure cuts, policies that Britain can effect in
its own short term as well as long term interests to promote
development. These have to do with the use of North Sea oil.
The effect of present practices is that we are holding our exchange rate at a level which is actually damaging parts of the
manufacturing sector of the economy, which should not be damaged
even within an adjustment context. We should not only be able
to make up the cuts in the development budget, but also massively
increase the real impact in the developing world by encouraging
an expanded overseas investment programme.

The second major area of concern is the Government's overall
trade policy, which can be summarized as follows: it is as
important as aid is for the stimulation of Third World trade,
through which the poorer countries can promote their own development. In spite of the energy crisis and fear of world recession,
the Government sees evidence of a move towards a more liberal
trading system rather than an increasing world wide protectionism,

as one might expect. In both the multilateral trade negotiations
and in the UNCTAD, developing and developed countries alike have
acknowledged that protectionism is no answer to the world
recession. Relief of poverty and stimulation of trade are
stabilising forces in a world which seeks peace and prosperity.
An important by-product is that we ourselves benefit from the
trade generated by the policies we pursue, by helping the Third
World to become less poor and more credit-worthy we protect
existing markets and develop new ones for British goods and
services. Trade is by its very nature a two-way process, and
those who still see assistance in the field of trade as charity
are taking a very short-sighted view. The British aid programme
is responsible for at least 50000 jobs in the United Kingdom
and it is up to British firms to take the opportunities available
to market their own goods and services in the developing world.

My own position differs slightly from this official Government
stance in so far as we can all agree in isolation that a liberal
trading regime is necessary and that trade with the developing
world is an important part of the development process. If we
are going to encourage private investment then obviously the
corollary of that investment is that we must be prepared to
accept the products that British and other investment produces.

The political reality of not only Britain but of the entire
developed world today is marked, in my view, by a substantial
and growing trend towards protectionism. Governments have
failed so far to offer a clear prospect of re-employment when
declining industries finally close. We have failed to convince
the textile workers of Lancashire, the steel workers of South
Wales and the shipbuilding workers of the North East that there
are alternative jobs for them. It is not surprising that they
hang on dearly to what they have got. In the context of South
Wales or the North East, arguments about spontaneous industrial
growth ring hollow in the background of unemployment rates
already well in excess of 10 per cent.

In fact, the case for protectionism has become very much more
politically respectable as a result of misinterpretations of the
case being advanced by Cambridge economists who argue for a
comprehensive series of import controls. Ironically, the most
implacable opponents of the kind of *ad hoc* import controls that
we have seen on textiles and footwear are precisely the economists of the Cambridge school who argue a case for import controls
on a totally different basis and wish to operate it in a totally
different way. Winn Godley, who is the leading exponent of that
particular view, is firmly on the record as saying that import

controls do more damage than good if they are done simply as a
response to political pressures in declining industries.

The pressures in developed countries for protectionism potentially represent enormous damage to the developing world; but
they are pressures which exist and which have to be met head on
because the problems which bring them about are real problems,
human problems just as much as the problems of underdevelopment.
If we accept the case for global development and the concomitant
case for adjustment within our own industries here at home, the
Government itself has an important role to play in defining the
context in which that adjustment will take place. It is not
enough simply to leave it to the market and to say that the
market forces will allow the declining industries to decline
and now industries to come in their place.

The Government itself must articulate a coherent development
policy — including trade measures — that involves more than
simply signing a cheque for £850 million annually for the
developing world. More comprehensive policies are required if
Britain is to adjust to the world economy and to new economic
realities. In this respect, the Brandt Commission is wrong in
arguing that this must be done by all the twenty rich countries
of the world operating together. Waiting for twenty rich
countries to operate together provides nineteen excuses for
inaction. The best way, and indeed the only way, of getting
this programme on the road is for individual national governments — which are still, whatever we may think to the contrary,
the only source of legitimate power in the developed world —
to take the future of their own countries and people in their
own hands. While certainly they must discuss what they are
going to do with their colleagues, they must also do something
about it themselves.

In making this call for Government action, I would not hesitate
to use the word 'planning'. In contrast to prevailing wisdom,
it has an impeccable Tory pedigree. There is no better analysis
of the scope for Government action and planning in this field
than Harold Macmillan's *The Middle Way*. He addresses precisely
the issues that we are talking about now and criticised the
Tory governments of the late 1930s for not adopting precisely
the kind of strategy that would have fitted then and is still
relevant now.

While it is not within the power of the Government to create
large numbers of jobs, it can ease the process by which jobs
are created, and that is where the planning process comes in.

As an illustration, I would like to refer to my own experience, when I worked in the clothing end of the British textile industry. I was at that an unwitting participant in the development process.

There is a clear indication of what can be achieved by comparing the British and the Dutch clothing industries. If 1970 is considered as 100, British clothing output now stands at 112; we have actually boosted output in an industry for which there is only an extremely limited future in this country. In Holland that same index now stands at between 50 and 55. A very substantial reduction in their clothing output has thus taken place over actually quite a short period; the unemployment rate in Holland is now lower than it is in Britain and the average rate of wages higher.

The key argument about rich country interest is to provide people with alternative work outside industries like clothing, textiles and shipbuilding. Jobs should be created in higher-value-added industries, where more skills and more advanced processes are necessary and where higher wages are possible than in declining traditional industries. A similar experience to Holland's has also occurred in Germany and Japan. We have all heard about the threat that Korea poses to steel and other basic industries. If Korea imposes a threat in Western Europe, how much bigger a threat does it pose to the same industries in Japan? However, if one examines the trading relationships between Korea and Japan, Japan is one of the very few countries in the world which has run a balance-of-payments surplus with Korea. Japan has allowed some of its industries to transfer the 500 miles across the water to a much lower wage economy and has itself been strengthened in the process.

The third central element of Government policy in the Third World relates to the role of foreign investment. The present Government believes that private investment can and should play a greater part in development. Exchange controls have been relaxed, which should help British firms to transfer capital overseas as portfolio investment is totally free. Developing countries should thus have increased liquidity based on private investment in spite of the continuing dangers of nationalisation, expropriation and changes in taxation law. Limiting or removing these dangers through the negotiation of an investment promotion and protection agreement, which provides a real legal framework within which bilateral investment can develop, would further stimulate investment and the present Government is actively pursuing such agreements. Developing countries should accept

that it is in their interest to improve the climate for investment by making sure that there is no sequestration of investment
assets and that there is no nationalisation without prompt,
adequate and effective compensation. While it is difficult to
generalise about the effects of private direct investment to
the developing world, private flows certainly have crucial functions to perform alongside official development assistance.
One advantage of direct foreign investment is that it carries
no fixed debt service obligations for the host country.

I would add little to this position with which I wholeheartedly
agree. However, it is important to emphasize that the government does not want a guarantee against nationalisation. However,
if a developing country wishes to attract private sector investment, it is reasonable that the Western company should get fair
compensation for the investment that it has undertaken if the
country then wants to nationalise it for its own internal reasons.

Finally, the Government's overall views on the Third Development
Decade could be summarized in the following manner. A realistic
assessment of the ability of the industrialized countries to
contribute to the development process cannot simply ignore the
constraints imposed on national policy by current levels of inflation, unemployment and growth. A great deal of work has been
done on the construction of economic models which indicate how
fast the economies of the developing countries can hope to grow
given ranging sets of assumptions. Realistic growth targets,
based on meaningful assumptions, can help to make the new International Development Strategy a powerful instrument for economic
growth in the Third World, and serve to maintain within the
industrialized countries the necessary political will to support
the development process. But there is a danger that unrealistic
targets based on assumptions which bear no relation to the real
world will discredit the strategy and tend to produce the
opposite effect. The responsibility for development is a joint
one between the developing countries and the developed world;
but the developing countries themselves have the primary responsibilities for promoting their own development.

The Government's position thus strikes very much the same chord
as the Brandt Commission when it underlines the importance of
having concrete programmes. They should be agreed among people
who can actually carry them out rather than resort to the kind
of resolution-passing which has tended to typify many United
Nations assemblies. Whatever programme we may agree upon to
promote the development of the Third World during the 1980s, it
should be based upon a realistic programme and not simply upon

targets and resolutions which salve peoples consciences, but which don't actually get effective action and produce results.

I have indicated the general lines of Government policy toward aid, trade and investment as well as how my own views coincide or differ. In many ways official policy has been almost totally unaffected by the thought and work that has gone into the Brandt Commission and the production of its report, in particular the interests of rich countries themselves in working toward the realisation of many aspects of the New International Development Strategy for the 1980s. British economic problems and individual government policies must be set within the context of a coherent overall strategy including an adequate response to the challenge of development in the Third World.

Much of the debate about appropriate responses is dominated by the moral case for promoting development. I must be forgiven as a politician if I make the point very firmly that in order to implement new policies those of us in the House of Commons must sell them to our electorates as something that is realistic and not going to damage their interests. While the moral case is important, the most important arguments of all are those which emphasise the unity of economic interests between the developed and the developing world.

In fact, whenever I talk about this subject I avoid using the word 'aid', because it has all the connotations of the fifties and the sixties. At that time, development was seen largely as charity, a yearly cheque signed by the British people to salve their consciences for the fact that they are richer than the majority of people in the rest of the world. In order to be sold in the United Kingdom, new measures on behalf of developing countries must be seen as part of a much wider policy to ensure the development and the growth of the world economy as a whole.

While it is overworked as a precedent and analogy, I nonetheless wish to suggest the similarity between Britain's position today and that of the United States in the late forties. The clearest and strongest argument that can be advanced for evolving a coherent policy for international development is based on the fact that there is a very strong parallel between today's Western economies whose traditional industries are no longer competitive because what they produce can be more economically manufactured in developing countries.

In many ways a similar position was the American one after the

Second World War when suddenly the 15 per cent of their national
production that was devoted to war was no longer necessary. As
Mother Courage said in Brecht's play, "Peace had broken out
again". An alternative use for war production capacity had to
be found; and General Marshall proposed that Europeans should
be provided with the ability to buy the products that Americans
were able to make. The rich countries now have a vested interest in pursuing the same strategy in order to provide developing countries with the opportunity and the wherewithal to
purchase the capital goods and the expertise that we should be
able to sell to them. Within this framework, there should be
little problem in persuading the British people to support the
kind of aid, trade and investment-based policies so necessary
to the United Kingdom's Third Development Decade.

CHAPTER 5

Management and the Third Development Decade

K. DURHAM

INTRODUCTION

Unilever is a large group operating in over 75 countries, many
of them in the category of developing countries. The products
that we manufacture and sell are pretty basic, being in the
areas of hygiene and food, agribusiness and chemicals. I
suggest that these are probably more important early indicators
of economic development than the prestige sectors of stripped
steel mills or nuclear reactors which some developing countries
appear to feel are evidence of their progress.

We have a long, and I believe distinguished, history in both
developed and developing countries not merely in manufacturing
but in the whole process of business activity. This ranges
from developing the use of indigenous raw materials through the
training of management to organising effective distribution.
The nature of our business, which is largely in consumer non-
durables, requires that we have to know the local marketplace
well and to understand its fundamental requirements if we are
to be successful in satisfying the needs of that market.

Because we supply such basic needs of the community, it seems
to me to be imperative that we are involved in, and indeed
stimulate, local development. After all, if you double the discretionary income of a German it is hardly likely he will wash
more or eat more, but if you double the discretionary income of,
say, an Indonesian he is likely to want, and to be able to pay
for, those things which we supply and which I believe satisfy
his deepest needs. The essentially local character of our
businesses means that we have to go beyond mere technology
transfer and have to train not only the local labour force but
also the management to a level every bit as good as that of

expatriate managers. And so we participate in and indeed benefit from the development of the economy of our host countries.

This then is the framework of my experience and the background
for my comments on the Third Development Decade (DD III) and the
contribution which business might make to the development of the
less fortunate countries.

ROLE OF UN AND OTHER AGENCIES IN PLANNING AND ECONOMIC GROWTH

The tragic condition of many of the world's inhabitants is un-
deniable, nor can we pretend that the 'gap' in living standards
between these people and those of us in the western democracies
is narrowing. All of us must earnestly desire to see the lot
of the unfortunate people in the developing countries dramatically improved. The problems we face are formidable. There is
no simple, obvious, solution or solutions. The question is how
best we can set about developing an effective response to these
problems.

Let me briefly comment on what is being done or, perhaps more
accurately, what we are all exhorted to do, to ensure that some
progress is made towards the real economic growth of the
developing countries. We are told that there must be a global
strategy for development drawn up and administered by national
and/or supranational agencies. There is, underlying much of
this planning activity, a belief that somehow or other centrally-
directed bureaucratic agencies know how to solve these global
problems. There are a variety of such agencies all having the
best of intentions and all genuinely desiring to improve the
situation; unfortunately, many of them have a poor track record
as far as stimulating economic growth is concerned. This is
hardly surprising because everywhere we see that Government has
been incapable of fashioning solutions to national problems and
this failure is merely compounded at the international level.
The arrogance of those who believe that supranational agencies
have the skills and abilities to alleviate global problems is
only surpassed by the size of the problems themselves. The
fact is that as we enter the Third Development Decade, in spite
of all the exhortations, planning, do-gooding and well-wishing,
the 'gap' is wider and is widening. There are more hungry,
ignorant and endangered children and adults than ever before.
And we also see that the target of international assistance is
further from implementation than when it was formulated.

Indeed, I would suggest that if progress has been made at all
it is largely because the professional managers from private
enterprise have been able, in spite of the constraints formulated by sincere but incompetent (in these matters) bureaucrats
and politicians, to make some relatively small but important
project work. A global strategy devised and administered by
some supranational agency is a mind-boggling concept. But it
is more; it is a dangerous absurdity because it would involve
implicitly the temptation to eliminate the proven advantages
of a free market system of supply and demand allocation in
favour of some bureaucratic and directing body.

The initial optimism about the value and contribution of global
strategies is now beginning to change into outright pessimism.
Ernst Michanek, the Swedish diplomat who has devoted a lifetime
to various planning and development bodies and who was involved
in the elaboration of all the United Nations' Development
Decades, has recently taken a hard look at what he labels the
'smokescreen' of international rhetoric: "If the proof of the
pudding is in the eating, we have now had enough. As I see it
today, we have got more pudding than strategy. The revolutionary
strategists — and I was amongst them — did not move the main
forces of development."

Many distinguished people, especially planners, have done much
to foster and popularise the concept of a homogeneous world of
less developed countries with essentially similar problems,
when in reality they are a diverse group with different problems
requiring local or national solutions.

As the planners have just completed setting out 'the strategy'
for the Third Development Decade, is it too much to hope that
some realism can seep into their consciousness? If they will
look at the reasons for the existence of the 'gap' they will
see that the market economies of the democratically governed,
industrialised nations have created more prosperity and enhanced
the overall well-being of more people in the past two generations
than has any other political/economic system. Why then, can
these planners not harness this free enterprise system? Why
should 'the plan' not embrace co-operation with (not coercion
of) the free enterprise system and allow it to produce the
effect which they so evidently have failed to promote? Whether
they like it or not, there is available to us now the most
effective engine for wealth creation yet devised. It would be
a tragedy if it were so 'cabined, cribbed and confined', that
it were unable to make its real contribution. That contribution

could well have as its main component the ability to tailor
solutions to problems rather than to insist on some uniform
response to all.

THE CONTRIBUTION OF PRIVATE ENTERPRISE

You will misunderstand my argument if you think that it is
based only on a poor view of human nature manifest in politicians and bureaucrats. Our worst enemies are not bad men
but rather ill-formed ideas about the institutional and legal
framework in which conflicting individual purposes can best be
reconciled and enabled to flourish in prosperity, peace and
freedom.

As I have indicated, we have tangible evidence of the ability
of companies — large and small — profitably to reconcile these
potentially conflicting aims and aspirations. Now I recognise
that it is not for the company, however large, to determine
'the national interest'; that is the proper and legitimate
role of Government reflecting, as far as it can, the real
aspirations of the people. Within that framework the company
should — and eventually must, if it is to succeed — perceive
the needs and scope of the market and through competition
satisfy those needs efficiently and at sensible costs. In the
real world of business competition people vote every day with
every purchase.

At present the contribution of British companies to the
economies of developing countries is considerable, although it
might be better. Britain is second only to the United States
in the extent and value of overseas investments. Of course,
there are those who believe that this outflow of capital from
Britain has been a major reason for the country's economic
decline. There is absolutely no evidence for this view; quite
apart from the considerable income remitted back into Britain
from overseas investment, the most successful British companies
tend to be those with international interests. The need to
adopt the best technology, to have good management and a well-
trained labour force, are essential requirements of international
competition and bring benefits to the parent country as well as
to the host countries.

I think the image of the British-owned company in developing
countries is good and I believe we have a better record than
most in developing indigenous management, in training the workforce, and in providing better and improving conditions of

employment. My observations indicate that British managers have
the ability, derived perhaps from their colonial heritage, to
blend with or to reflect local customs and culture; if you like,
to understand and fit in better than most. This quality is an
important foundation on which to build our contribution to
development and growth.

Barbara Ward has suggested elsewhere that a kind of 'Marshall
Plan' is needed to support developing countries. This seems
wide of the mark to me. The recipients of Marshall Aid all had
skilled, educated and literate workforces and an experienced
cadre of managers fully capable of immediately employing the
resources, financial and material, made available to them. Nor
is the improvement of developing countries to be achieved purely
by a redistribution of global wealth in their favour. We
already have the experience of many OPEC nations to show us that
mere transfer of wealth cannot guarantee productive application
unless there is a populace and infrastructure organised and able
to receive it.

Of course, one can argue that aid from United Nations agencies
or the richer countries has a major role to play although
experience has shown that official aid is often wastefully
applied, frequently misdirected and occasionally wilfully misused.
But even so, it seems to me that the concept of aid or redistribution of wealth as an important element in narrowing the gap
between rich and poor is misplaced. Any attempt to promote
international equality by wealth transfer would merely produce
a transient effect. Those factors which produced the inequality
in the first place would quickly reassert themselves and the
differences would reappear. But this would not be the only
defect in this proposition; it involves in essence a dilution
of the whole wealth-creating mechanism since wealth transfer
would divert resources from those who have demonstrated a
capacity to use them productively to those who use them less so.
What the developing countries need is a package that comprises
knowledge of raw materials, technology, ability to manage the
available resources, marketing skills and distributive
capabilities. These elements, when put together in a 'custom-
designed' package, have an integral quality to them such that
the final effect is much greater than the sum of the individual
parts of the package.

Some years ago, Daniel Patrick Moynihan, then the US Ambassador
to the United Nations in New York, reviewing the need for various
types of transfer to help developing countries remarked that

there appeared to be an existing institution entirely suitable
for the purpose. "It is", he said, "the multinational corporation". It seemed then, and still does seem, a most reasonable
suggestion to me. There are over 1000 British-based multinational companies and they represent a major resource to be
harnessed by developing countries.

Most multinationals engaged in manufacture overseas do make
appropriate transfer of resources in the form of a suitable
package. Certainly, out of self-interest, they develop local
men and women not only as a skilled labour force but also to
manage their companies in the host country. Regardless of the
motives (and I consider that wealth creation is a sound motive)
the results are a trained workforce and a managerial group for
the host nation. James Lee, President of Gulf Oil, encapsulated
my views when he said that "when the multinational is permitted
to operate in enlightened self-interest, it can enhance the
economic destinies of both the developing and the developed
countries. To do so, it must observe three responsibilities;
it must do its job well, it must earn a profit, and it must
operate within the constraints (economic, social and ethical)
of its host countries".

My theory, then, is that the developing countries have much to
gain by exploiting the capability of the multinational corporation. Perhaps it will be better here to omit the pejorative
word exploitation and to say that they would gain by enlisting
the co-operation of the multinationals. But alas, in spite of
the logic of using multinational corporations as a spearhead
for economic development, many developing countries are
suspicious of and resent the multinationals. The market economy
is under attack in many countries and the multinational is the
institution most often pilloried. Paradoxically, a major
complaint is that we are too efficient at our job of wealth
creation!

I am making the proposition that the greatest contribution to
the growth of the LDCs will come from business and particularly
from the multinationals. I think, therefore, it might be helpful
quickly to look at the reasons for suspicion and thereby try to
see a way to more productive co-operation. No doubt one of the
reasons is that the multinationals, or their predecessors,
arrived under the banner of the colonial power; even US multinationals are seen as an extension of the Western colonial
capitalism. The size of these corporations is also seen as a
threat, particularly to the local entrepreneur, whether he is

large or small. This threat is not just one of bringing better
technology, but also of marketing skills. For some reason,
there are many people (and not just in LDCs) who see marketing
as synonymous with exploitation, totally missing the point that
good marketing is needed to develop both the market and the
distribution system in precisely those remote areas that need
the product most.

Then there is a vociferous left-wing lobby which is against all
business, certainly big business and especially big foreign
business. The multinational is, of course, a natural target
for this group with the 'spectre' of dominance by foreign
capital as a rallying cry. After all, for a committed communist,
the success of a multinational might result in an established
successful capitalist society and the corporations are, therefore, to be feared and constrained. I tend to think also that
local politicians and bureaucrats feel uncomfortable with
multinationals. The latter after all are interested in results
in the foreseeable future; they are flexible, decisive and
efficient — qualities rarely if ever fostered by bureaucracies.
It is not surprising then that civil servants and their masters
prefer the multilateral agencies rather than the multinational
corporations. Then there is also the question of national pride
which is understandable and, certainly not unique to developing
countries.

Naturally, you could not expect me to agree with the image which
all these factors project of the multinationals. The absurdity
of the generality of a homogeneous group of developing countries
has an equal in the same generality for multinationals and I
do not accept that we are all alike. What we have in common is
an ability profitably to transfer know-how. Nevertheless, I can
still understand and have some sympathy with the worries I have
mentioned. It is unfortunately true that a few (a very few)
instances might be cited where the activities of one or two
companies have been less ethical than they should have been.
This suspicion has, together with ill-defined comments on the
economic power of the multinationals, given rise to a well-
orchestrated demand for the control of the corporations. I
have to say that this great economic power which apparently puts
us beyond Government has never been able to prevent any tiny
country which so desired from confiscating all our assets with
minimal or sometimes no compensation.

Nevertheless, codes of conduct have been drawn up by bodies like
the Organization for Economic Co-operation and Development (OECD)

and others which have been largely accepted by the multinational
corporations even though in their operation they may be harsher
than the conditions applied to local businesses — a situation
which we resent and which, if persisted in, will militate against
economic growth.

I welcome the recent Brandt Report which defines the problem of
the developing countries and its dimension with unusual authority
and compassion. It must have found a resonance with all of us.
It makes the moral case for help eloquently but also develops
the practical case for a redress of the economic imbalance.
Whilst the analysis is excellent, unfortunately I found the
recommendations disappointing. Once again we are to have recourse
to exhortation and the multilateral agencies; indeed to all the
things that have patently failed to work before. We already
have tangible evidence that this kind of aid does not hold much
promise of success. What a pity that virtually no mention was
made of the potential contribution of private enterprise except
to suggest constraints or codes of conduct. It is a damning
commentary on these statesmen that, of all the experts they
consulted, virtually none were businessmen or industrialists! Can
we not from this give the message that business has, if not the
most, certainly one of the most crucial roles to play in promoting
growth.

Let me illustrate once again the enormous educational and
attitudinal problems that confront us. While the Brandt Commission was sitting we were subjected to another conference of
these multination groups with its impractical demands. I mention
it only to indicate the artificial difficulties which are being
quite needlessly promoted. At the most recent UNIDO conference
in New Delhi in January 1980, developing countries once again
confronted developed countries. To effect transfer, the 'Group
of 77' asked for an annual outlay of $4 billion and unlimited
access to the developed nations' information systems, both
Government and private. This was clearly unacceptable not only
to the Western democracies but also to the Soviet Union and its
satellites. Moreover, the demands were presented without any
supporting statements about the nature of the projects to be
undertaken or the agency that would distribute the funds. An
attempt by the US Government to clarify the position merely
resulted in arguments on protocol and organization structure.
Such failure to recognise the realities of the problem and to
recognise the contributions already made mainly by multinational
corporations is unhelpful, especially when it is allied to non-
negotiable demands.

Now I would be the last person to argue that private enterprise companies are perfect; after all, I know them better than most of you do. But I am quite certain that private enterprise companies and particularly, by nature of their structure and knowledge, the multinational corporation, will be the most effective agencies for achieving what we all desire — a significant increase in the well-being of all the less-well-off nations. I recognise the worry that such nations have about us and certainly we must do our best to alleviate those worries. I also recognise the need to ensure that our behaviour must be acceptable to the host nations; indeed, I believe it largely is. But if we are to make progress there has to be a greater receptivity and co-operation from the developing nations. Political instability and a sharp adversary approach to both Western democracies and the multinational corporations are not conducive to progress. Nor is the economic relationship and co-operation that is needed helped by the formation of blocs, unreasonable proposals in the United Nations, refusals to join in realistic proposals for investment protection, or the creation of some nebulous international bureaucracy which controls neither the sources of new technology nor the corporations with the capability of transferring it.

But there is, as I have mentioned all along, considerable grounds for hope. The engine for growth and wealth creation is at hand! Some progress has already been made in meeting the economic development needs of some developing countries as shown by the newly coined description of some countries as 'NICs', referring to Newly Industrialised Countries like Brazil, South Korea, Taiwan, and so on — and this is largely because they have actively enlisted the aid of private companies. There are others who are beginning to realise the role which private enterprise and foreign investment can play in the development of their economies and who are giving encouragement to such institutions to help them help themselves. If we can bring together Governments, agencies and companies in a co-operative mode rather than a confrontational mode, then the objectives which we all have can be realised. It may take some time to attain them, but with the right attitudes they are visibly attainable. That surely is a more sensible way than the elaboration of a global strategy which can hardly be understood let alone implemented.

CHAPTER 6

Trades Unions and the Third Development Decade

JACK JONES

The slow progress on North-South problems has been due, in my
opinion, to the rarefied atmosphere in which the discussions
have taken place. An elite of governments, politicians, civil
servants and academics have all been involved. I would not
question the need for all of them to make their contribution,
and many have done so with sincerity and distinction. There
can be few with humanitarian feelings who would question the
need for political leaders at the highest level to get their
heads together as has occurred in the Brandt Commission. But
the Brandt Commission and the elite who have been concerned
have generally not, at any stage in my experience, taken up the
issues with ordinary people.

Until the North-South dialogue becomes a popular issue there
will not be the impetus, nor the thrust and urgency in outlook
required to reach the peak of the mountain; and I don't mean the
highest peaks but some of the smaller ones on the way to the
highest peaks. I submit that the trade unions can and should
play a key role, and to a degree they are already making a small
but important contribution in many practical directions. That
they represent an enormous potential for spreading knowledge
and arousing interest and support must be obvious. Yet, to a
very great extent, they have been ignored. Outside of the
International Labour Organization (ILO) and a few international
organizations, their voice has been hardly listened to. Even
when they make representations, the response from authorities
tends to be slight.

This is not to say that the trade unions are doing all that
they should. They certainly are not. They, like other sections
of the community, must be persuaded to try harder to make the
problems of developing countries clear to the masses in the

developed countries. Trade unions should be decisively involved
and positively assisted in an all-out effort to make the issue
open and clear to working people in general.

CORRECTING MISUNDERSTANDINGS

My personal concern to arouse the public interest of ordinary
people is not new, but it has been restimulated by reading,
some months ago, a book published in 1978 by the Ministry of
Overseas Development, then headed by Judith Hart. The book,
A Survey of Attitudes Towards Overseas Development, was aimed
both to test the public's knowledge and understanding of overseas aid and development and to provide an indication of its
attitude on these issues. Interviews were conducted over a
cross-section of nearly 1000 adult British citizens. The most
significant of its findings implied that not only was the size
and real cost of public spending on overseas aid virtually
unknown to the general public, but even the terminology of
development was hardly understood. Many of those interviewed
thought that the Third World had some reference to "UFO".

The weighted average of the public's assessment of national
average spending by the British Government was 70pence per head
of the population. In fact, that was 3.5 times as much as the
real figure (20pence). When told what the government actually
spent, no fewer than 69 per cent of those interviewed said that
the figure (70pence) was about the right amount or that more
ought to be spent. The inference seems to be that, with a
little effort, the British government could gain support for
spending much more in development aid. Instead a substantial
cut in aid expenditure has been effected.

This shameful situation makes it all the more necessary that
the public conscience should be aroused. One clear feature that
emerged in the report is that people feel they do not know very
much about aid and development. When the position was explained,
the responses were generally sympathetic. One person said:
"To me, somehow, that 20pence there stands out and makes one feel
feel very small. It makes me want to take back some of the
things I was saying earlier". Many of the those interviewed who
came down in favour of more aid did not feel that it gave or
should give Britain either political or economic advantages.
It is important to consider such views in the light of recent
references by certain ministers who say: "If we're going to
give aid we must have advantages for it; there is nothing wrong wit

using aid as a weapon". Well apparently the public is not really
very favourable to that sort of attitude.

More people gave humanitarian and 'one world' views as reasons
for supporting aid rather than justifying it by pointing to the
trade benefits which it might bring. One of the main conclusions
expressed by the author of the survey (Mr. T. S. Bowles) is that
"the present results suggest strongly that the correction of
common misunderstanding about aid expenditure could directly
influence level of support for this expenditure."

In other words if we could find a way of getting over to the
people just how little we contribute to Third World development,
that in itself would begin to evoke among the people a feeling
that a lot more could and should be done. Last year Britain's
development aid amounted to 0.39 of one per cent of its gross
domestic product, about half of the United Nations target of
0.7 per cent. So we are a long way behind the figures we
apparently agreed to in the international assemblies in terms
of what we do.

This correction of common misunderstandings is surely a job for
all of us. That is why I say it should be made a people's
issue. I have no doubt that the attitude displayed in Britain
also applies in most of the other nations of the developed world.
Something, a big something, must be done about it. It is not
sufficient to have great national and international figures
sitting down in massive assemblies. Perhaps they ought to assist
in bringing the issues, the information, the assessments home
to the people. And, not least of all, the media should be a
focus of activity. Surely not only the *Times* and the *Guardian*,
but also the popular press can use their skills to facilitate a
more widespread understanding of this humanitarian issue, to
overcome the misunderstandings. It could be done, and yet they
gave so little publicity even to the Brandt Commission. There
were other things that day. Kevin Keegan was being sold to
another club and so on. But it seems to me that there are so
many people of good will at every level who ought to be able to
persuade the bosses of the media that they at least can do one
or two acts of goodness in their life; and this is one of them.

Schools are very important too. Anyone interested in education
must agree that children's understanding of this problem is
absolutely crucial, because they can go back to their parents
and their families with new ideas, as well as of course building
for the future a better understanding of these problems. But
the strongest effort must come from political leaders, from

church leaders, from opinion leaders everywhere and not least
from the trade unions. They must be encouraged to do more; they
must be prodded and pressed into doing more. I know that they
get criticized a lot and maybe justly. Having been in the forefront of criticism from time to time, I tell you that criticism
in the newspapers and in public is a helpful way of getting a
consideration of the problem. So I'm all in favour of prodding,
or putting the spotlight on people. That is why I say that
unions and the rest must be persuaded to do more.

STRONG REASONS FOR AID

Of course the humanitarian aspects should be at the forefront
of this battle to improve the lot of the poor millions in the
Third World, but there are also very strong material reasons for
a new economic order; and these reasons should be put to the
people in clear and unmistakeable terms. Not so very long ago,
I heard the Prime Minister of Sri Lanka state: "The interdependence of our economies is such that if we falter, we will
not be able to buy the goods you produce. Our poverty, which
in many cases we have learnt to live with, will inevitably pull
you down as well". That message needs to be relayed to all the
people in the developed countries and the trade unions can play
a very effective part in conveying that message.

In particular, Britain and other developed countries are becom-
ing increasingly dependent on exports to Third World countries.
About 30 per cent of the exports from the EEC countries go to
the Third World, and there are a lot of jobs in countries like
the United States and Britain involved. While this is not the
main issue, we ought to correct the idea that the growth of the
developing countries is a threat to us, because in general it
is not. A new body like the Commonwealth Trade Union Council
has an important role to play in this respect.

In general, the international trade union movement has failed
to achieve popular understanding of Third World problems,
partly because of the inadequacy of rank-and-file participation.
It is true that international trade union conferences do provide
an opportunity for trade unionists from the developing countries
to meet together and to work together with their counterparts
in the industrialised world. The President of the International
Confederation of Free Trade Unions (ICFTU) is from Malaysia.
An Indian national is one of the leaders of the World Federation
of Trade Unions (WFTU), and people from the developing countries
play a strong role in the leadership of the World Confederation

of Labour (WCL). However, full-time people at the top of their trade unions are not always linked closely with working people in their own countries.

An individual can become very remote and lose contact with workers' consciousness. It is about people, about the rank-and-file members, not about the glory of this, that and the other top individual. Courageous efforts have been made by trade unions in a number of developing countries, particularly Latin America, in trying to improve the lot of members as well as in fighting for elementary rights. Trade unions thus contribute to improving the general position of developing countries. In this respect, we should not underestimate the strong opposition to the efforts of trade unions in many of these countries from unsympathetic governments and employers. Opposition has often meant death and imprisonment for large numbers of trade unionists.

The stronger trade unions of the Western world could do a great deal more to assist the trade unions in the Third World in strengthening their membership, in overcoming the fragmentation and disunity which too often exists and in doing everything possible to assist the unions in undertaking their tasks against almost impossible odds. Little is known about the efforts of these trade unions in trying to carry out their essential role of resisting exploitation and improving living conditions and working standards. Creating, organising and extending trade unions is a massive task in the developing countries, particularly because of the essentially rural character. Yet unions are badly needed to secure improved living conditions and to monitor aid to see that it is used to relieve the poverty of the people. Trade unions of the Third World which work effectively represent a challenge to inefficiency and corruption.

The words spoken about Indian government aid schemes by a Mr Raj Krishna, in his presidential address to the Society of Agricultural Economics of India a few years ago, are very relevant: "Instead of reducing the poverty and idleness of the poorest, it may further enrich the rural oligarchy and bureaucracy, and increase inequity and tension in the countryside. The unemployed, the landless, the crop sharers and the insecure tenants must be organised into strong unions to demand that project funds and benefits really reach the poorest, and are not swallowed up by contractors, rich farmers and petty bureaucrats. Without militant rural unionism, aid policies have not benefitted and will not benefit the mass of the rural poor."

Certainly rural trade unionism would help the drive for a more
practical approach to rural development in the Third World. I
have been told by many trade union sources that there are too
few middle level managers and local leaders for rural development and too little international effort to produce them. This
important middle link, practical local management, is too often
missing. One report I have seen said: "We need fewer planners
and more practically trained men prepared to work in the countryside. Many of the planners are working on false statistics,
because when urban educated people are asked to do rural work,
finding out what's happening in rice production or family planning, they simply make the answers up. So you don't need to
take notice of those fancy computer results; they have no
relation to reality."

A realistic approach is vital and that is why the ICFTU in its
voluntary aid schemes in rural areas has tried to develop co-
operative arrangements, involving the rural workers themselves
in the leadership of projects. Much of the premature mechanis-
ation in some rural areas of the Third World led to a lot of
distress in driving large numbers of peasants to the squalor
and poverty of cities that could have been avoided had the rural
workers themselves been brought into the picture at the earliest
possible stage.

VOCATIONAL AND TECHNICAL TRAINING

The shortage of technicians and tradesmen in rural areas is also
true of the towns and industries of many developing countries.
Extensive efforts to produce more technicians and tradesmen are
a priority if progress is to be achieved because vocational
training schemes are an important element in self help and in
ensuring self-reliance. It is a form of aid in which trade
unions can join forces with governmental and non-governmental
agencies. Experience of technical and trade training schemes
are relevant and the 'know how' could thereby be made available
quickly.

Even if a 'brain drain' results (and we know that in many
countries, including Sri Lanka and Mauritius, skilled tradesmen
have gone into the Middle East and are getting a good living
because they have got a trade that the Middle East wants and
can pay for), no one should stop short the process of training.
Experience shows that there can never be enough technically
trained people. Development plans are too often held up by

technical failures or breakdowns due to a lack of technical and practical expertise. Due to such problems I personally have seen power stations out of action in Guyana, buses off the roads in Trinidad, and new container cranes not operating properly in the ports of various developing countries.

Apart from technical assistance, it is necessary to ensure that the transfer of technology to developing countries takes the social interests of the working people fully into account. Any stimulation of the national economies of developing countries naturally requires some advanced technology. It is clear, however, that not all such technology creates employment; in fact, it has resulted all too often in the destruction of jobs. The transfer of labour intensive technologies should thus be encouraged, and Third World trade unions should be consulted. The impact of the technology to be utilised on the employment situation should be fully taken into account in order to avoid the prospect of a massive loss of jobs in a situation that is already wrought with high unemployment and underemployment.

Particular attention should be given to the protection of the health and safety of workers. It is in these areas where the trade unions of industrialized countries can be a great deal of practical assistance to their counterparts in the Third World. The provision of adequate research support is also an essential ingredient in this respect, and a bit of this sharing has started. Trade union centres in countries like Guyana, Jamaica, and Mauritius, where I have been recently, are beginning to ask for and receive some research help from the international trade union movement and bodies like the Trade Union Congress.

The intention would be to enable trade union movements in the developing countries to participate more effectively in the development progress of their countries in the following ways:

(1)   to influence social and economic policies

(2)   to undertake research to meet the specific as well as the general needs of the trade unions

(3)   to further collective labour bargaining and to improve labour relations

(4)   to assist the development of worker participation, industrial democracy and worker co-operative experiments

(5)   to provide expertise in economic analysis to the trade unions

(6)   to advise on the nature and availability of technical and
      vocational training schemes and means of effecting the
      transfer of 'know how'

(7)   to enhance the capability of the trade union movement, to
      respond to as well as to provide social and labour
      legislation.

As developing countries grow, it is vital that they should have
adequate information concerning safety and health legislation,
based upon the experience of the trade unions in developed
countries. Yet I want to see two-way exchanges between trade
union representatives of developed and developing countries.
There is nothing that brings home understanding better, more
clearly and more sharply than direct personal contacts. I don't
just mean the top trade union leaders. I think that there is a
tendency to move in elite circles without really touching the
problem. I would like to feel that more and more ordinary people
from Britain would be meeting their equivalents in the developing countries, from the grass roots. With a bit of pressure
and encouragement from management and the trade unions, more
men and women from the shop floor would go and meet their
counterparts and begin to discuss how we can gain a better
understanding of development problems. We could open the prospects for better understanding; it would be part of the clearing
of the misunderstandings that I've mentioned; and it would
accelerate the pace in overcoming the North-South stalemate.

CONCLUSION

Experience shows that this approach cannot be left to the trade
unions alone. They have got to be pressed, and they will need
the help of governments and non-governmental organisations.
There is certainly a case for an agreement on common efforts
between the churches and the trade unions. The powers that be
will not do very much unless they are pressed to do it and
pressed to do it in a sense by their constituents. If Members
of Parliament start to get approaches from tens and twenties of
their local constituents, they begin to sit up and take notice.
We have got to make that sort of activity widespread as a means
of advancing enlightenment and understanding, correcting common
misunderstandings and making sure that people of good will everywhere begin to open up this vast issue of how we reduce the gap
between rich and poor nations. The elmination of world poverty
is a long process, but it is worthwhile attempting. We can

indulge in rhetoric, we can indulge in phraseology; but we have
got to begin to grapple with the problems of development
realistically. It requires a combined push by all of us — and
if we make that push, we can transform the situation tremendously.

Trade Unions and Global Development

CARL WRIGHT

INTRODUCTION

The Report of the Independent Commission on International
Development Issues, the Brandt Report on the North-South disparities in the world, serves to underline the extent to which
the world is divided into 'haves' and 'have-nots'. The notion
of two worlds, to adapt the concept of two nations, is not new
to the trade union movement. Trade unions have come about as a
result of the inequalities in society, and owe their origin to
the refusal of working people to take their fate lying down.
They were established so as to create a new economic and social
order in society, which would ensure a fair distribution of income and wealth.

It is tempting to draw the analogy between the struggle of the
trade unions on behalf of working people and the struggle of
the developing countries for a new international economic order
which seeks to effect a fair international distribution of
income and wealth. Indeed the Group of 77 developing countries
have sometimes been termed the 'trade union of the world's poor'.
Certainly there can be no mistake about the glaring inequalities
between the rich 'North' and the poor 'South', in terms of *per
capita* incomes; in terms of industrial production; in terms of
the basic indices of elementary human requirements, such as
food, clothing and shelter; to say nothing of essential community services.

The international power structures, largely the result of the
post-war reconstruction period, when few developing countries
had achieved full independence, and of the unparalled growth of
large transnational corporations, are no longer adequate to cope
with the tasks required of them. The aim of the United Nations
Third Development Decade Strategy must therefore be to help
build new structures, suited to the world of the 1980s and 1990s
and based upon the UN's proposals for a New International
Economic Order.

The attitudes of certain advanced country governments when faced
with the demands of the poor countries however seem to display
the same unyielding and narrow-sighted inflexibility that the
landed gentry and the industrialists of the nineteenth century
displayed to the early trade unions. Here again parallels exist.

The analogy between the trade union movement and the Group of 77
developing nations should not however be taken too far. Even in
the most wealthy countries of the world, there remain substantial
areas of poverty and deprivation, as well as resistance to social
change and progress. Indeed a number of investigations have
shown that the real gap in income and wealth distribution has
narrowed little, even if there has been an increase in prosperity
in an absolute sense. Sometimes, too, governments seek to
reverse history and to destroy the achievements of the past.
In the developing countries, moreover, there is much inequality,
and while there are notable exceptions, internal distributions
of income and wealth leave a great deal to be desired, the
result of unequal patterns of land ownership, or massive accumu-
lation of wealth by local elites.

ECONOMIC REVIVAL

The UN's Third Development Decade Strategy will encounter major
difficulties unless the world is able to pull out of the deepening recession. Ever since the 1973-1974 slump, the trade unions
have argued for a positive economic strategy, aimed at restoring
growth and creating new jobs. Government policies, especially
those of the main developed countries, have however had the
opposite effect and the world economy is in the worst shape it
has been in since the Great Depression of the 1930s. There are
now over 20 million workers without a job in the OECD (Organization for Economic Co-operation and Development) countries
alone — to say nothing of the 300 million who are unemployed or
underemployed in the developing world, whose lot is the most
severe of all. Inflation, far from being controlled by demand-
cutting policies, is spiralling upwards, and the outlook for the
immediate future is grim.

The economic policies which have emerged in particular since the
1979 Tokyo Summit, and were reaffirmed at the subsequent meeting
of the IMF (International Monetary Fund) and World Bank in
Belgrade, reflect only pessimism, uncertainty and a lack of
direction. It is, moreover, absurd to imagine that in a highly
complex world, economic management can be based purely, or even

largely, on the quantity of money and rate at which that money
circulates within the economy. Indeed the actual application
of monetarist policies in a number of countries is showing that
it has done little or nothing to reduce prices, but has had a
disasterous effect on growth and jobs.

The trade unions do not accept that holding down prices and
creating employment are conflicting objectives. Given the mix
of demand management and supply management, both can be achieved.
Just because traditional remedies have not been succeeding does
not mean that they should be disregarded; they need to be built
upon and adapted to the changed circumstances, taking into
account the real forces that shape the economy, notably market-
dominant companies.

More than a piecemeal approach is required. Bold and imaginative
initiatives are called for, and the leading developed countries —
the United States, Japan, the Federal Republic of Germany, the
United Kingdom, France, Italy and Canada — as well as the other
OECD countries, have a special role to play. It is essential
that these countries co-ordinate their economic strategies — as
they were beginning to do in Bonn in 1978 — with a view to
stimulating global growth. Unless this is done, mass unemployment and the accompanying social and political problems will
become a permanent feature of the 1980s and will thwart any con-
certed effort at an effective international development strategy.

MUTUALITY OF INTEREST

The developing countries can, as the Brandt Report highlighted,
play a central role in the revival of the world economy.
Already they contribute massively to world economic expansion,
being a major market for goods and services of the developed
world. Thus in 1977 the US, the EC and Japan sent more than
one third of their exports to the developing countries. US
exports to the developing countries were more than four times
their exports to Japan and nearly twice those to the EC with
the result that one job in twenty in the US is production for
export to developing countries. EC exports to developing
countries are three times those to the US and twenty times those
to Japan; moreover, in 1975 they increased at a time when exports to developed countries decreased. In contrast, and despite
what is often thought, the developing countries share of the
markets of developed countries is, with the exception of certain
sectors, very small indeed. Given the enormous latent demand
in the developing countries the potential for expansion, if

living standards could be raised even by only a small degree,
is vast.

The mutuality of interest between developed and developing
countries calls for a major initiative to raise living standards
in the less prosperous parts of the world. What is required is
a 'world development plan', to be launched by the developed
countries to provide assistance. This plan should aim at helping the poor devote more resources to building up a domestic
market and boosting internal levels of demand. Such a project
would be in harmony with the objective of greater global balance
in demand and supply and would make a major contribution towards
the recovery of the world economy. As an immediate step, the
world development plan should involve action by the developed
countries' governments to honour the target of 0.7 per cent of
GNP as official development assistance within the short term —
say the next two years — and to raise it to 1 per cent within
another two years. In addition, active consideration should be
given to launching some form of 'development tax', as advocated
by the Brandt Report.

POSITIVE ADJUSTMENT POLICIES
AND FAIR LABOUR STANDARDS

A further factor inhibiting change is the frequent absence of
positive adjustment policies, or the failure to endow such
policies with the necessary resources. The Brandt Report states
quite explicitly that "the record of industrial adjustment
policies is not very satisfactory." Where workers have confidence in the ability of governments to provide alternative jobs,
resistance to change will be substantially reduced. Positive
adjustment policies must therefore be pursued with vigour by
the governments of developed countries and be endowed with the
necessary resources.

Workers in developed countries must be able to see that any
measure of solidarity does in fact benefit their follow workers
in the developing countries. The Brandt Report has rightly
pointed out that "unions raise questions when they suspect that
wages in developing countries are being held down by exploitation of a weak and unorganized labour force, by excessive
working hours, or by the use of child labour. They resent it
all the more if the competition makes excessive profits —
especially if it comes from multinationals, which in some cases
may also be their own employers."

Measures must consequently be taken to ensure that workers in
the developed countries actually benefit from adjustment. In
this context, the Brandt Report has stated that "Fair Labour
Standards should be internationally agreed in order to prevent
unfair competition and to facilitate trade liberalisation" and
has pointed to the long-standing demand, supported by trade
unions on both developing and developed countries, for the in-
clusion of a 'Social Clause' in the General Agreement on Tariffs
and Trade which would aim at helping to guarantee respect for
the Fair Labour Standards of the International Labour Organization (ILO).

ENSURING THAT THE PEOPLE BENEFIT

The ordinary man and woman must secure real benefits from
economic change. This is why the international trade union
movement insists on a new social as well as a new economic order.
It is to be welcomed that during the 1980 discussions on the New
International Development Strategy, the Group of 77 developing
countries placed major emphasis on targets for reaching full
employment, eliminating hunger and malnutrition, reducing and
eliminating poverty and bringing about a fair distribution of
the benefits of development; also on universal education, decent
health facilities and the availability of basic shelter. The
satisfaction of such essential needs is vital in any development
strategy and policies towards meeting those needs will have the
strong support of trade unions everywhere.

Policies for creating employment and satisfying the basic needs
of the people should form the core of the Third Development
Decade Strategy and should be translated into concrete activity
at the national level. Such policies were set out in detail in
the Programme of Action, adopted by the 1976 ILO World Employment Conference and revised by the ILO in 1979. In this connection it is worth recalling the recommendation of the 1979 International Labour Conference, endorsed by governments, employers
and unions from both developed and developing countries: namely
that governments should, at the national level, "formulate, as
appropriate and in close co-operation with employers' and
workers' organizations, both quantitative and qualitative targets
in order to implement an employment generating basic-needs
strategy. Such targets could have different time perspectives
and could, for instance, specify the number of entrants to the
labour market which should be absorbed into employment, the
rate at which existing unemployment and under-employment should

be reduced and the rate at which the incomes of the poorest
groups should be increased, in order to improve their relative
positions."

POPULAR PARTICIPATION

It is essential that there be full and effective participation
by the entire population at all stages of the development
process. Practical experience has shown that trade unions and
rural workers organizations can, at the national and international level, play a major role in helping the fulfilment of
developing objectives. One area is in dealing with transnational
corporations, where, in the discussions on a UN Code of Conduct,
the trade unions have argued for the establishment of information
and consultation mechanisms which would allow workers' representatives from developed and developing countries to meet together
and present their views to head office management.

Indeed it can be argued that only by marshalling large and
representative sections of the population, as are represented
by workers' organizations, will development objectives be fully
met. In this connection, it is worth once again refering to
the Brandt Report, and to the introduction by the former
German Chancellor, in which he solemnly declares: "International
social justice should take into account the growing awareness of
a fundamental equality and dignity among all men and women.
Scientific, technological and economic opportunities should be
developed to allow a more humane social and economic order for
all people. Strong efforts should be made to further a growing
recognition of human rights and of the rights of labour and
international conventions for protecting them."

THE ROLE OF THE CTUC

These are the issues — equality within nations, as well as
equality between nations — which form key concerns of the
Commonwealth Trade Union Council (CTUC) which formally came
into existance on 1 March 1980. It is the aim of the new
Council to promote the interests of workers in the Commonwealth
through enhanced co-operation between national trade union
centres; to present views to Commonwealth institutions and
governments; and to promote acceptance of, and respect for,
trade unionism and for the Commonwealth Declaration of Principles
of 1971, which sets out the basic relationship between Common-

wealth countries. Thus for example, special attention has been
given to practical ways in which the emerging trade unions in
Zimbabwe could be assisted. At a more formal level, a meeting
has been held with Mrs Indira Gandhi, Prime Minister of India
and Chairman of the 1980 Meeting of Commonwealth Heads of
Government of the Asia-Pacific Region, to present her with
trade union viewpoints.

Underlying these aims is the firm belief that trade unions have
a positive contribution to make to the achievement of new
economic and social relationships, at the international as well
as at the national level. The commitment of the trade union
movement to the United Nations' proposals for a New International Economic Order is on record. In so far as there is
any qualification, it is that the fruits of the new structures
and relationships must accrue to the ordinary man and woman,
and not to rich elites or big corporations. Trade unions in
both developed and developing Commonwealth countries will therefore seek to promote the goal of economic and social development of a progressive kind. Equally they will make their voice
heard if development is of a retrogressive nature; to do otherwise would be failing in their duty to their own members.

CHAPTER 7

Christians and the Third Development Decade

Christianity and Global Development

RIGHT REVEREND R. RUNCIE

In the 1950s, when I was teaching in a theological college, one of the subjects on the curriculum was 'Mission Studies'. It was an optional extra, and very few students took it. The others called them 'empah wallahs'. For we hardly needed the Suez affair of 1956 to remind us that the sun of the British Empire was setting at last, and that we could no longer think of exporting our faith under the shadow of the Union Jack. The important thing then for the coming generation of Church of England clergy was to find a way of making the faith relevant in the dechristianised society around them. For most, that was bounded by the Straits of Dover; only the more venturesome looked beyond for inspiration, to the Mission de Paris or the witness of the Church amidst the 'Wirtschaftswunder' — economic miracle — of West Germany. The Alps were the furthest horizon. What was happening across the Mediterranean, in Africa or in Asia, let alone in the *terra incognita* of Latin America, lay beyond all ken.

So we regarded, for instance, as slightly dotty the works that were beginning to pour from the pen of a former Coal Board economist, E. F. Schumacher. Nor did we include on any list of required reading such books as that published in 1960 by the veteran Christian historian Professor Herbert Butterfield, *International Conflict in the 20th Century — a Christian Perspective*. We should have done well to take note of what he had to say:

> "There is no realm of life which calls for profounder re-
> thinking than that of international affairs; — no realm where
> it is more necessary to do hard things with our personalities,
> unloading ourselves of former prejudices and piercing through
> successive layers of insincerity."

97

For the 'hard things' Professor Butterfield offered hope:

> "It may be a prejudice of mine, but I wonder whether Chris-
> tians, if they could disentangle their minds from the con-
> ventional mundane systems that constrict them, might not,
> within a decade, contribute something creative to this deeper
> cause of human understanding."

Within a Decade, another book by Professor Butterfield was
published in the year that the United Nations had named as the
start of the First World Development Decade and in the sixties
there were some signs of creative Christian contribution to the
development debate.

In the Anglican Communion, the Toronto Congress in 1963 was a
landmark; it came out with the phrase "Mutual Responsibility
and Interdependence in the Body of Christ" (soon shortened to
M.R.I.) making the novel suggestion that giving should not all
be from the 'haut' North to the 'bas' South. Rather, the
established churches of the northern world should expect to
start receiving from the churches of the South whatever it was
that they had to contribute, and, only through the unfamiliar
process of receiving, learn afresh how to contribute themselves
to what Marshall McLuhan suddenly taught us to see as 'the
global village'.

More recently this kind of thinking, and a concern for world
development, has become our orthodoxy. At the 1978 Lambeth
Conference, readily enough 400 of the bishops signed a letter
to express our solidarity with the suffering in the threatened
South African township of Crossroads. South Africa is easy
game. We were put more on our mettle in Canterbury that summer,
when a television company came and said that they wanted to give
the conference serious attention, and what would we do? So some
three dozen of our number, under Archbishop Coggan's chairmanship, staged a 90-minute debate examining just these matters,
and the programme went out under the title 'Religion or
Revolution'. It is as stark as that, nowadays.

It was not only Anglicans who caught this new vision. The
Second Vatican Council reflected it very broadly with such
documents as the Papal encyclical *Populorum Progressio* and the
establishment of a Pontifical Commission for International
Justice and Peace. The World Council of Churches also kept
hammering away at the priority of God's concern for equity
amongst the nations of the earth. That ecumenical pioneer,
Bishop Leslie Newbiggin, has chronicled these hammer-blows in

the preparatory document he wrote for the 1980 World Conference
on Mission and Evangelism, *Your Kingdom Come*. He traces how
the weight of Christian concern has moved from preoccupation
with personal salvation and morality to a sense of corporate
salvation for humanity. In the global — literally ecumenical —
process there is a central place for world development. Describ-
ing the Fourth General Assembly of the World Council of Churches,
held in 1968 in Uppsala, Bishop Newbiggin puts the new emphasis
in a powerful Biblical simile:

> "The churches, which often seemed to belong rather to the
> court of Pharaoh than to the camp of Moses, were summoned to
> identify themselves unequivocally with the aspirations of the
> oppressed."

Indeed, for the Judaeo-Christian tradition in which we stand,
the book of Exodus provides a classic text for the Church called
to distance itself from 'conventional mundane systems'. In
particular, an archbishop of an established church must find
himself constantly addressed by the narrative of the commission-
ing of Moses. I look at Chapter 3 of Exodus, and find, wedged
between the two revelations of God — the conventional 'God of
Abraham, God of Isaac and God of Jacob' and the new and awesome
'I AM THAT I AM' — a passage of four verses threading one, two,
three, four, five strong active verbs:

> "I have seen the affliction of my people ..."

> "I have heard their cry ..."

> "I am come down to deliver them ..."

> "I will send thee unto Pharaoh ..."

> "I will be with thee ..."

I read the Book of Exodus, and I read the Brandt Report.

> "I have seen their afflictions"

It was, I gather, only when the members of the Brandt Commission
held one of their meetings in Mali, amongst the poorest of the
world's very poor, that their intelligence and their passion
fused, and North and South came to write with a single voice.

> "I have heard their cry."

The cry of impoverished people is not for charity. It is for
justice. No, we need not subscribe uncritically to the Second

World view, somewhat reflected in the Brandt report, that the former colonial powers carry exclusive blame for past exploitation, and the burden of responsibility for putting things to rights. Yes, we cannot be deaf to that cry. We hear it, not as Christians in a vacuum, but as citizens living within an economic system still geared to exploit the world's poor. It is a cry for big deeds to get the natural wealth of the poorer world reinvested where it belongs.

"I have come to deliver them"

In Jesus, born in a cowshed and tucked in hay, Christians believe that God has come down to deliver. Jesus lived rough, therefore can we be complacent about our comforts, or should we be hearing what the liberation theology of Latin America has to say about deliverance, and about the way we live? Ages ago, Jeremiah saw the hand of God moving, with majestic improbability through the actions of Cyrus, king of Persia. Since 1973, we have had our chance to detect the hand of God moving through the equally improbable agency of the oil sheiks. Now, after oil, comes grain. Frederick Forsyth's latest bestseller, *The Devil's Alternative*, based its plot on the failure of the Russian grain harvest. What, I have to ask myself, is God's alternative, and how can the Church be His improbable agency in a world where the USSR does indeed have to bargain for grain from North America, grain for fattening meat that the Poles don't have; and where there are rumours of crop failures in China, and even that tiny kingdom of Lesotho, en-isled by South Africa and once proud exporter of grain, now has to buy-in its bread at the rising market price?

"I will send thee unto Pharaoh"

Yet any thought of personal austerity is pointless unless as citizens we press our governments, and through them, the supra-national and international agencies, to take such action as renegotiating the terms of world trade. To introduce, for example, further world commodity agreements, like that on cocoa, which is now beginning to do something to make a base for prosperity in West Africa. To fit ourselves for such action means that we have to learn the language, and that is not easy. The jargon of "SDR's" and 'UNCTAD' and so on does not come naturally to the average parish representative on the deanery or diocesan synod. But then what language did the Good Samaritan have to master, to communicate with the man he helped or with that unsung, trustful intermediary, the landlord on the Jericho road?

For us now the Pharaoh to whom we are sent is easy enough to identify by the Mercedes in which he rides. He (or she) may be a director of a multinational corporation, an international bureaucrat, a member of government. Or he may be a superior electronic salesman, relying upon defence contracts for his bread and butter, and then, for his jam, selling his technology at the expense of employment, and ancillary to that, in Taipeh, in Sao Paolo, as well as in Coventry.

That reflection on Exodus 3 brings E. F. Schumacher back from the periphery into the ranks of the major prophets of our times. He is not by any means the only one. Another economist of Capetown University, in a study he prepared for a Partners-in-Mission consultation, has drawn attention to yet one more bad consequence of the dominance our system allows to the multi-national corporation. Instead of spreading wealth, their activities suck it all into what he calls an urban core economy, so hastening the impoverishment of the rural homelands.

Again, it is easy to point a finger at South Africa, but what is happening there is true on a larger scale elsewhere. What was once described as the golden coffin, a rich trough of North-western Europe lying between Manchester and the Ruhr, now perhaps only across the Channel, has the same effect upon the nations of the European Economic Community, already including Greece and shortly to include Spain and Portugal. In good times, the 'Gastarbeiter' come to where the work is. When times are bad, they are the first to get the sack, and left to go home empty-handed.

Knowing that our manufactures depend more and more upon — to use the ugly catchphrase — capital-intensive technology, at the expense of a greater and greater proportion of the workforce, Christians cannot naively applaud the creation of wealth. Nor is it enough for us to be latter-day Luddites and deplore the microchip. If anything, we have to be prepared to examine the axiom that we have accepted uncritically from Engels and from Marx, that work — the cash nexus of employment — is the defining activity of human beings in an elaborated society. It could be a Christian function to proclaim, not only for long industrial-ised societies but for the world at large, that leisure and communications are properly at the centre of our common dealings. Indeed, something of this sort may for our age be a revelation of what we understand from Scripture about the nature of a three-in-one God, busy from Sunday to Friday and resting on the Sabbath.

Given its secular premises, the Brandt Report falls short by
not looking seriously enough at the question of work, employment
and leisure. It does, quite rightly, concentrate upon the need —
if we are not all to go bust — to move things south. In this
period of world recession, that is what economists with a
Christian stance must be ready to tell Pharaoh. In the last
great depression, fifty years ago, that great Christian social
thinker Reinhold Neibuhr wrote that the churches needed more
than a blueprint of the Promised Land; to achieve it, they
needed to be partners, on proper terms, with those who had the
power to help them get it. The same is true now.

So much for Butterfield's 'hard things'. Now to his hope. It
was at the end of the First United Nations Development Decade,
on the eve of the Second that could so easily have been jetti-
soned, that the churches of this country showed they had got
the message. In December 1969 they sent a petition signed by a
million Christians, urging that 0.7 per cent of the Gross
National Product of the United Kingdom be allocated in official
government aid to developing nations. Ten years later, it was
no longer just a matter of centrally organised petitioning.
Seven hundred towns and villages across the country organised
events in connexion with the work of the Churches' Committee of
the World Development Movement's third One World Week. I heard
some members of a branch of the Church of England's Mothers'
Union being interviewed on B.B.C. radio. They had been playing
the Grain Drain, a game that Christian Aid had produced to set
people thinking how things happen. These Mothers' Union members
had learned their lesson: quite simply they explained, as they
now saw it, how free market forces help the rich and hurt the
poor.

The Brandt Commissioners intended that their report should prod
ordinary people into action — schools, trades unions, Rotaries
and Round Tables, churches, women's groups, yes, and the Mothers'
Union. With my own past involvement in broadcasting, as chairman of the Central Religious Advisory Committee, I am particularly excited by the opportunities on offer from the new Channel
Four, when it starts transmitting in Autumn 1982. For the first
time in the UK, it enables church bodies of one kind and another
to fund and make a direct contribution to the output. So I am
especially interested to learn that various Christian bodies are
associating themselves with the activities of the Fourth Channel
Development Education Group, a conglomerate that aims to provide
a regular strand of programmes focussing attention on the positive side of world development. It will be a change from
starving babies, earthquakes and famine, which till now have been
the things that make news.

Any Anglican clergyman often finds himself pronouncing an elaborate form of blessing: "The peace of God, which passeth all understanding, fill your hearts and minds with the knowledge and love of God". I am happy enough to say that, but I have sometimes wondered how peace is supposed to induce knowledge, let alone love. I have learned a lot from Professor John Macquarrie's book, *The Concept of Peace*. Peace is only possible, he argues, when all the constituent members of a society, and of a family of nations, are striving to fulfil the potential that remains to be developed and realised within them. This is both the peace we seek, and the peace that, as Christians believe, is Christ's gift to those engaged in Exodus with him. In a hurry to escape, we read in the book of Exodus, the children of Israel had no time to spare for frills, so they baked their bread flat. Week by week, day by day, Christians break that flat bread together, and it tells of a hungry world in a hurry, and of a God who is powerful enough to save, if only we will dedicate to His service, ourselves and our grain and the wine that bubbles over with mirth; and even the water of the United Nations Drinking Water Decade of which we are mostly made, and without which we die.

The Churches and the Third Development Decade

CARDINAL BASIL HUME

The Christian Church, of its nature, has to concern itself not only with its pilgrimage to the Promised Land and securing the Kingdom of God, but it has also to contribute to the building of the earthly city, the daily affairs of men and women.

When the Second Vatican Council reflected on this twofold concern, the bishops declared:

"The work of Christ's redemption concerns essentially the salvation of men; it takes in also, however, the renewal of the whole temporal order. The mission of the Church consequently is not only to bring men the message and grace of Christ, but also to permeate and improve the whole range of the temporal ... The layman at one and the same time a believer and a citizen of the world, has only a single conscience, a Christian conscience; it is by this that he must be guided in both domains." (Decree on Laity n 5).

It is, then, legitimate for a Christian and a Churchman to
concern himself and to interest others in the problems involved
in the Third Development Decade.

We cannot be committed to the values which should prevail in
our society, such as the upholding of human dignity, freedom,
justice, peace and fellowship, unless we study those things
which militate against them and devote our energies to removing
them.

There are at least six dangers which threaten human values in
our modern world. Some of the problems have been with us for a
long time. There is, however, today a sense of urgency. The
former President of the European Commission, Mr Jenkins,
recently warned us Europeans: "It is now certain that if we do
not change our ways while there is still time — and 1980 could
be almost our last opportunity — our society will risk dislo-
cation and eventual collapse." The Brandt Report — *North-South:
A Programme for Survival* — sees the next twenty years as fateful
because many global issues will come to a head. I have referred
to the Brandt Report; it is an important contribution to any
serious debate concerning the future of our society.

The six issues which I believe to be destructive are these:

(1) The great disparity of wealth among nations is obvious
     from the fact that 800 million people are officially
     designated as 'destitute'. UNICEF estimated that 12
     million children died in 1978 from hunger. There are in
     all about 2000 million poor people, most of them outside
     the global trading system. And this great disparity in
     wealth separates, generally speaking, the rich but econ-
     omically stagnant nations of the North, from the poor and
     developing countries of the South.

(2) The threat to the environment in which men and women must
     live from the wholesale pollution of land, sea and air.
     The Brandt Report claims that "global pollution and
     exploitation of atmosphere, soil and seas ... amounts to
     plundering our planet" and asks, "Are we to leave our
     successors a scorched planet of advancing deserts,
     impoverished landscapes and ailing environments?"

(3) Linked with this ecological problem is our failure to
     control the energy resources of the world. It is well
     known how unbalanced is the use of energy. As the Brandt

Report says, "It is no exaggeration to describe this
(energy problem) as an emergency. There is no need to
dwell on the dangers that lie ahead: the vulnerability of
supplies to political upheaval in any producing country;
the threat of major hardships for developing countries;
the dangers to the world economy — not to speak of the
even greater dangers of possible recourse to military
intervention by major powers who see their vital interests
at stake in any serious disruption of supplies."

(4) The potentially catastrophic effects of nuclear war have
been reported by the Brandt Commission: "It is a terrible
irony that the most dynamic and rapid transfer of highly
sophisticated equipment and technology from rich to poor
countries has been in the machinery of death." And, as
Earl Mountbatten said in Strasbourg on May 11, 1979: "In
the event of a nuclear war, there will be no chances, there
will be no survivors — all will be obliterated, so I repeat
in all sincerity as a military man, I can see no use for
any nuclear weapons which would not end in escalation,
with consequences that no-one can conceive." The relationship between disarmament and development is clear. Current
total expenditure for military purposes is approaching
$450 billion a year — half of which is spent by the Soviet
Union and the United States; while annual expenditure on
official development aid is only $20 billion. It is
obvious that if even a fraction of the world's annual
military spending were diverted to development, prospects
for the poorer countries would be vastly improved.

(5) The problem of hunger is perennial and is closely linked
with the previous point. "While hunger rules, peace
cannot prevail" says the Brandt Report. It also points
out that "morally it makes no difference whether a human
being is killed in war or condemned to starve to death
because of the indifference of others." Food is an
absolutely basic human need; are we unable to satisfy this
need for so many millions of people in this twentieth
century? We do not lack the technical means of eliminating
hunger and poverty. Do we lack the will? Can we generate
the sort of global compassion that will induce us to part
with material resources, to lower our standard of living
in order to release resources for those in such dire need?
The record of international aid so far is not encouraging.
It is many years since the United Nations voted that rich
countries should each give 0.7 per cent of their annual
income to aid poorer countries. In Britain this would be

70pence in £100 ... and we do not do it. In fact most western industrial nations give well below this amount to development programmes. Meanwhile thousands die of hunger.

(6)   The failure to respect life is the final destructive issue. The cruelty and insanity of the Nazi holocaust and the Stalinist regimes have not deterred latter-day dictators and fanatics. This technological and rational age has created victims on a scale that daunts the understanding and dulls the imagination. Human dignity and rights, human freedom are under constant threat from regimes — both East and West — which refuse to recognise the inalienable rights of the individual. Innocent human life is respected only if people are strong enough to resist in defence of their rights. National security, liberation movements, the implementation of Marxism, are all considered by interested parties to be enough justification to deny individuals their God-given right to live. This contempt for the individual, subordinates the person to the system, the State, the Creed. It poses a major threat to true development.

Each of these six points — and I am sure readers could easily add to the list — raises moral problems. They are not simply matters internal to any country, nor matters of national defence and economics, nor are they neutral issues. The questions they pose should challenge the conscience of every human being. The solutions to the problems are, in different ways, and in varying degrees, the responsibility of each one of us.

As I reflect on the six threats to human development, I have to conclude that each one constitutes a collective sin; a social or institutional evil in which the sinfulness of the world is clearly demonstrated. They provide for me powerful proof of humanity's fall, which is not to say, of course, that each of us is personally at fault, nor do we each stand guilty before God. But humanity's tragic legacy does demand that humanity as a whole should take responsibility for its future destiny.

Most of the evils I have described are well-documented in the Brandt Report. The Commission on International Development Issues makes recommendations for future action. We may decide not to agree with the solutions proposed. But as nations and as individuals we should think about them and reject them only in favour of better solutions.

The Brandt Report should be welcomed. It is making us face up
to the crisis of our generation. Solutions will be hard to
accept and may be fiercely resisted. There can be no excuse
for retreating into our national or sectional 'bunkers' in a
last-ditch defence of our narrowly conceived self-interest.
Political 'realism' or expediency should not blind us to the
need for sacrifice and effort. Nor should the pursuit of the
ideal be naive and simplistic.

Most people are rather good at spotting the weaknesses in others;
they can easily analyse their shortcomings or pick holes in
their arguments. It is easy to criticize society and to point
out evils and abuses. It is quite another matter to make a
positive approach, to discover an ideal to inspire human living.
And this is badly needed today. The Brandt Report says: "New
generations need not simply economic solutions, but ideas to
inspire them, hopes to encourage them, initial steps to implement these ideas and hopes."

The Christian religion is not concerned only with warning us
about the dangers and the reversal of fortune embodied in the
story of Dives and Lazarus. Christianity is also concerned
about effective action — to clothe the naked, feed the hungry.
But even this is not enough. Our faith goes further. It is a
reaching beyond self, a striving for that which is above and
beyond merely human accomplishment. It is a desiring to go
further than the limits of human experience. It is the exploration of the mystery which is God and the glory of man redeemed.
That, too, is part of the programme, and its implications will
and should occupy us endlessly. It is a specific contribution
that we of the Christian family can make to the future of
humanity. It is that vision of what man is and what he is for,
a vision that is difficult to discover unless set in the context
of that vital relationship of man to God. For Christians, it is
in Christ, God and Man, that we shall discover the ideas which
will inspire, the hopes that will encourage and the ability to
take those steps with Him who is the Way, the Truth and the
Life.

The Third Development Decade: a Christian Responds

BARBARA WARD

The reactions of Christians to the great issue of international
social justice must inevitably be rooted in the Gospel and the

words of Christ. Perhaps the best starting point is the parable
of the Good Samaritan. There, you will remember — I paraphrase
a little — a lawyer, trying to put Jesus to the test, correctly
answered Our Lord's question: "What is the basic moral law?"
The man replied, "To love God with your whole mind, heart and
spirit and to love your neighbour as yourself." Our Lord
commended him. But he seemed ready to deepen his understanding.
So he said "Who is my neighbour?" Then Our Lord told him of the
Jew who fell among thieves on the road from Jerusalem to Jericho.
They robbed him, wounded him and left him in the ditch. A
priest and a levite 'passed by on the other side'. Then a
Samaritan took pity on him, bound up his wounds, set him on his
horse and took him to an inn and paid all the expenses. "So",
said Our Lord, "Who was neighbour to him?" And the lawyer
replied, "Why, he who showed compassion." Christ replied, "Go
thou and do likewise."

In other words, the essence of neighbourliness is rooted in
compassion, in the ability to see fellow human beings as
'other selves' with the same needs and troubles as our own.
From this follows the duty of active pity and equal justice.
We should know this, of course, from almost every page of the
Gospel. Not only have we Our Lord's own example in healing the
sick, comforting the afflicted and feeding the hungry but in
His picture of the final judgement it is precisely those who
feed the hungry, shelter the homeless, clothe the naked and
visit the sick and the imprisoned who will be welcomed into
eternal life.

We have, too, the other darker side of the parables, Dives
condemned for his greed and his indifference to destitute,
ulcerous Lazarus starving at his door, or then the man who used
a larger harvest to build bigger barns and settle down to enjoy
himself. But the Lord said, "Thou fool, this night thy soul
will be required of thee." No, there can be no dispute here.
A basic commitment to social justice is the key to the moral
life. We must love our neighbours as ourselves or any claims
we may make to love God are quite simply empty.

The evidence from the Gospels is universal. Yet I think we
should reflect a little further on the good Samaritan. The
Jews despised and scorned the Samaritans. There was no sense
of family or tribal or national affiliation. The Samaritan
acted because he saw a suffering man who in human terms could be
said to be absolutely alien to him. Is there not a reminder
here that our compassion must not be confined to family or
group or nation but must reach out to all mankind? The starving

child in Bangladesh is my neighbour as is the deprived child in
a British slum. Pope Paul VI expressed this fact in that basic
document of international social justice, *Populorum Progressio*,
when he said: "The social problem has become worldwide." Pope
John Paul II repeated the judgement in his address to the
United Nations in 1979. "Economic development, with every
factor in its adequate functioning must be constantly programmed
and realized within a perspective of universal joint development
of each individual and people, as was so convincingly recalled
by my predecessor, Pope Paul VI in *Populorum Progressio*." This
papal teaching, inevitably, reflects the Gospel's main thrust —
that we must see social justice in a universal perspective,
passing beyond local and national frontiers. Our 'neighbour'
is everyone in need whom we can help.

Who then are the needy ones? In the last two years we have
received a massive up-to-date documentation on the basic
economic and social conditions of our world economy in *North-
South, the struggle for survival*, issued by a group of distinguished leaders from both the developed industrialized Northern
nations and the developing Southern part of our planet, meeting
under the chairmanship of Chancellor Willy Brandt. The facts
which I offer you to illustrate the state of our present international system are largely taken from this report. Three-
quarters of humanity (in the South) live on one-fifth of the
world's income. We, as British people, belong to the privileged
quarter of world population that enjoys four-fifths of the world's
wealth. In parts of Africa and Asia, some 800 million people
live on the very margins of subsistence with famine as a
citizen's constant threat and millions of children dying of
malnutrition every year. Yet in parts of the North, citizens
consume nearly a ton of cereals a year per person (largely in
meat equivalents) while millions in a land like India eat only
400 lbs a year in the direct form of grain.

Contrasts in the use of energy are as startling. One American
today (and Europe has been trying to catch up on American
patterns of consumption) uses as much commercial energy as nine
Mexicans, sixteen Chinese or over a thousand Nepalese. More
than ninety per cent of the world's industry is in the North
and almost a hundred per cent of advanced research and technological facilities. Yet many forms of disguised protection
prevent the poor from selling their cheaper goods in Western
markets. The cost of rising food and oil prices since 1973 has
catastrophically increased the poor South's load of debt. In
1970, it was $70 billion. Today it is over $300 billion and
inability to pay and difficulties in recycling such vast sums

threatens the stability of the whole monetary system. Above
all, this is not a static contrast. Over the next two decades,
nearly 2 billion more people will be added to the world's 4.4
billion, the great majority in the poorest lands. Can there be
any doubt who is Dives and who is Lazarus? The facts speak for
themselves and demand from every Christian, nay, from every
citizen of good will, a positive and generous response.

The Brandt Commission suggests a four-part emergency programme
to see us through the next perilous decades. First comes a
massive transfer of resources in capital from rich to poor.
The 0.7 per cent of national income promised by the rich in
1970 should be reached by 1985, bringing development aid up
from $20 billion a year to $50 billion. (If these figures seem
huge to you, remember the four hundred and fifty billion dollars
the world spends each year on arms, the most wasteful, the most
inflationary of all expenditures). The Brandt Commission then
proposes co-operation with the oil producers to develop an
agreed energy policy with a reliable price mechanism and among
the rich a wholly new emphasis on conservation.

The next point concerns the central need — reliable food
reserves and speedy agricultural development in the Third World.
We cannot stress too greatly this fundamental need for food aid
and development. Malnutrition is the greatest killer of the
young. As long as babies are expected to die, there can be no
solution to the vast surge of growth in the population of poor
lands. If parents still see death take their first offspring,
they will seek child after child as a sort of reinsurance. It
is where (as in the North and the more prosperous developing
lands) food, health, education and some hope for the future
have been achieved that a stabilization of family size has been
successful and this is where food supplies are critical since
malnutrition is perhaps the largest predisposing cause of in-
fantile mortality. In short, the only fundamental hope of
solving the population problem lies in a massive sustained
pursuit of development and social justice in the poorest lands.
For this reason, the Brandt Commission seeks to institutionalize
a fairer and more generous sharing of the world's resources.

The fourth point in its immediate strategy is to seek permanent
means of aid and transfer — for instance by a system of international taxation on arms — on some forms of trade. But clearly
the urgent point is the rapid release and transfer of resources.
This is the challenge to the rich countries. Are they prepared
to extend to all humanity the kind of sharing which, however
     ly, has helped to hold developed societies together in
     st half century?

No doubt we would all like to feel that human decency, some
sense of common obligation, some stirring of conscience would
be enough in our once-Christian West to produce the response of
compassion and generosity that are so urgently required. But
we must be realists. If such a conscience existed, it would
have stirred already. The parsimonious figure of less than
0.4 of one percent of national income — the present level of
most Western aid giving — would have moved closer to the
solemnly promised 0.7 of one percent. The repeated attempted
dialogue between North and South on the need for a 'new international economic order' would not have ended in the rejection
of genuine concessions by the North and growing acrimony and
impatience in the South. Nor is the mood likely to change when
the North, caught in a vicious spiral of rising prices and
falling production — our so-called stagflation — is more tempted
than ever to turn to the protective and destructive measures
which created the collapse of 1929. With unemployment at 18
million in the older industrialized lands and inflation rates
rising to 10 per cent or more, the cry of conscience has little
chance against those who say: we must help ourselves first.

But, here again, the Brandt Commission gives us a clue to what
may break the impasse of the wealthy nations turning to inward-
looking measures marked by an unchanging lack of generosity.
The whole thrust of the Brandt Report is to show that a
sustained, large-scale, imaginative effort to stimulate, render
productive and enrich the three-quarters of mankind that subsist
on barely twenty per cent of the world's resources would benefit
the rich nations fully as much as the poor who are being
assisted. As the report puts it: "The world economy is now
functioning so badly that it damages both the immediate and
longer-run interests of all nations. The search for solutions
is not an act of benevolence but a condition of mutual survival."

The reasons are obvious — but too little understood. How many
Western leaders, to give the most direct example, seem to
realize that at least one-third of all the merchandise exports
of the United States and the European Community have been going
to the Third World since 1973? If this vast market had not been
available, we should have had yet higher unemployment: at the
same time the so-called 'cheap imports' from the nations that
are industrializing in the South have helped to keep a damper
on some prices. If now, as the Brandt Commission suggests, the
potential purchasing power of the really poor were systematically
increased by providing the needed capital and skills, the markets
opening up to the older and more saturated but technologically
more adaptable Northern states would be an 'engine of growth'

to stop intolerable levels of unemployment and the steady rise
in inflationary pressure. Admittedly, the strategy requires a
measure of rearrangement of unemployment patterns in industrialized countries (so do silicon chips). But Holland and Sweden
are already preparing plans for a policy of technological re-
deployment and I have heard the report that no Swedish trainee
is out of work for more than six months.

Now, just in case you feel that this interpretation of how the
world economy might work is a foolish and irresponsible optimism,
let me remind you of something. In a world totally disorganized
and flattened by five years of war, the Americans' decision in
1947 to give away, for half a decade, two per cent of their
national income in the 'Marshall Plan' revived Europe, stimulated
their colonies, reversed the certainty of stagnation and at the
same time led to expansion and prosperity in America as well.
There are thus people living among us — and I am one — who have
seen two catastrophic periods in the world economy, the first
in 1929 when nothing was done that was not inward-looking and
ungenerous and led on to a decade of depression and war, and
the second in 1947 when American aid and vision turned out to
be enlightened self-interest and set the whole world economic
system working again. Clearly, what the philosopher Santayana
said is true: "Those who will not learn from history are destined
to repeat it." We can too easily forget the benign example of
1947 and reforge the fetters of 1929. It is in the profound
interest of all the nations that we make our choice for generosity, for sharing, for expanding markets by developing the
poorest countries and for a co-operative effort of North and
South together. This would build a world society in which
human respect, compassion and simple justice create the basis
for mutual love and peace — and with peace, some hope of ending
the disastrous race for arms.

We must grasp and underline this fact of mutual interest because,
as I have said, we do not command, even among Christians, a
sufficient number of committed citizens who will act on the
guidelines of conscience alone. As voters, we must make clear
to our elected representatives and to our Government that aid-
cutting and covert or overt protectionism are the old road to
disaster and that votes are at stake in rejecting or choosing
the return to 1929.

But do not for one moment think that the basic issue is not that
of social justice, human compassion and an active world-wide
sense of our common humanity. As Pope John Paul II expressed
it in his address to the United Nations: "Surely the only way

to overcome this serious disparity between areas of satiety and
areas of hunger and depression is through co-ordinated co-
operation by all countries. This requires, above all else, a
unity inspired by an authentic perspective of peace." Unity —
that is the key. Is it too much to hope that this generation
of Christians, particularly here in Europe which was once 'the
cradle of the faith', will see that their primary spiritual
task is to work for a united humanity? Will they be inspired
by the vision of a world community in which Christ's mysterious
image of himself as 'Son of Man' can be realized at last because
nations, peoples, tribes and families become true neighbours
and build together the social and economic foundation of a just
and hence a peaceful world?

CHAPTER 8

Summary and Conclusions

A. JENNINGS and T. G. WEISS

In each of the contributions there is a clear warning of the
dangers which face developing and developed countries if yet
another decade passes without coming to grips with the problems
of world poverty. Not surprisingly, the representatives of the
different interest groups express different views as to the
diagnoses of the problems and the prescriptions for their
resolution.

THE WARNING

The dangers which face developing countries in the forthcoming
decade are not new. Millions of children die of hunger each
year; UNICEF estimates that approximately 12 million children
die from hunger in an average year. There are in total about
2000 million poor people. Of these 800 million are officially
designated as 'destitute', constantly suffering from hunger,
disease and homelessness. Rampant inflation, massive unemployment and underemployment (300 million people are estimated to be
unemployed and underemployed), spiralling import prices, and
deteriorating export prices (with limited exceptions such as
oil) are threatening even the limited progress achieved to date.
The cost of rising food and oil prices since 1973 has catastrophically increased the poor South's debt burden. In 1970
it was $3 billion, and in 1980 it exceeded $70 billion. By the
end of the century it is said that there could be two billion
more mouths to feed, the vast majority of whom will be located
in developing countries; and even with successful expected
growth rates, the presently unacceptable number of destitute
will thus increase significantly. Human life, human dignity,
and human freedom will suffer on an increasing scale.

115

The poverty of the developing countries also endangers developed countries. Dividing the world into 'haves' and 'have-nots' generates political instability. The contributors to this volume and its readers belong to the privileged quarter of the world's population that enjoys four-fifths of its wealth. In parts of the rich North, citizens consume nearly a ton of cereals a year per person, (largely in meat equivalents), while the many millions in a land like India eat only 400 lbs a year in the direct form of grain. One American today uses as much commercial energy as one thousand Nepalese. Ninety per cent of the world's industry, and almost 100 per cent of advanced research and technological facilities, are in the North. Most of the armed conflicts in the post-war period have in fact occurred in poor countries, and there is a growing danger that such instability could spill over into a super-power collision leading to catastrophic, nuclear devastation.

As well as a danger, interdependence constitutes an opportunity for the rich. Despite their poverty, the poor countries play a major role in the economic well-being of the rich, as a major and growing market for goods and services. In OECD countries alone, over 20 million workers are without jobs, and one cannot ignore the fact that approximately 1.5 million jobs in the North result from trade in manufactures with developing countries. EC exports to developing countries are three times those to the United States and twenty times those to Japan. US exports to developing countries are more than four times the exports to Japan, and nearly twice those to the EEC; one in twenty US workers is employed for production for export to developing countries. Several contributors advocate the Brandt Commission's proposal to increase the potential purchasing power of the poor by providing them with needed capital and skills. Thereby an 'engine of growth' could be created to stop intolerable levels of unemployment and the steady rise in inflationary pressures in the developed countries.

A Christian dimension is added to those warnings arising from the mutuality of political and economic interests between North and South. As Barbara Ward so eloquently says, "the basic issue is that of social justice, human compassion, and an active worldwide sense of our common humanity." The reactions of Christians to the great issue of international social justice must inevitably be rooted in the Gospel and the words of Christ. Cardinal Hume does not mince his words when he warns that if humanity fails in the forthcoming decade to respond to social and institutional evils — including great disparities in wealth, hunger, environmental pollution, nuclear warfare, waste of energy resources, and failure to respect human life — humanity's tragic legacy of sinfulness will be repeated.

THE DIAGNOSES

The urgency of the warnings of dangers facing both developed and developing countries in the Eighties is a reflection of the failure to respond adequately to the challenge of development. One theme which runs throughout contributions is that a single split between North and South — developed and developing, rich and poor — is in fact misleading. It suggests a community of interests which does not exist in the real world. The so-called 'Group of 77' (developing countries) includes major exporters of industrial goods and recipients of foreign investment, other countries — the majority — faced with a battle of economic survival, and oil producers with large foreign exchange surpluses. The 'Group B' countries (western market economies) also exhibit a wide range of characteristics, including their orientations toward the issues of Third World development.

There is therefore no simple diagnosis. Indeed a summary by Professor Jolly of the results compared with targets set in the two previous development decades shows that the central goal of income growth was more than achieved during DDI, and only slightly underachieved in DDII. This aggregate average, however, conceals a well-above average growth performance by OPEC and newly industrializing countries, and a markedly below average performance by the lower income countries. Mr Weiss further notes that almost half of the thirty one structurally weakest countries, the 'least developed', have registered negative rates of growth in income *per capita* in the decade.

Notwithstanding this major reservation regarding the diversity of country groups, the following factors used to explain poor development performance in the first two development decades were highlighted by various contributors:

(1) Most significant is the disappointing aid-giving perfor-
    mance by the rich. A number of western countries (in-
    cluding Sweden, Denmark, Norway and the Netherlands), have
    attained the target of 0.7 per cent per annum of GNP; but
    the overall average is still only 0.3 per cent, indicating
    the very poor, and worsening, aid performance by some of
    the most important donors (USA, UK, West Germany, and
    Japan). The aid performance of the Socialist bloc
    countries has been particularly disappointing.

(2) Targets for trade expansion have not been achieved because
     of the dislocation to the world economy caused by the
     chaos in the international monetary system; primary commo-
     dity shortages and price fluctuations; general inflation
     (particularly oil prices) and recurrent slow-downs if not
     recessions; and the increase in protectionism.

(3) Failure of planners "to harness the free enterprise system
     ... as the most effective engine for wealth creation yet
     devised," is emphasized by Mr Durham. A concomitant theme
     underlined by Messrs Marten and Dorrell is the failure of
     many developing countries to have made private investment
     an attractive possibility.

(4) Failure to involve ordinary people in the issues of the
     North-South dialogue is emphasized by Mr Jones. The
     discussion has been restricted to elites of governments,
     politicians, civil servants and academics. The inter-
     national trade union movement has also failed to achieve
     rank and file participation in Third World issues. Lack
     of unionization in the Third World, particularly rural
     trade unionism, has hindered the spread of benefits to the
     mass of rural poor.

(5) Domestic economic policies may also have hampered progress
     in the North-South debate. Mr Wright agrees that "it is
     absurd to imagine that in a highly complex world, economic
     management can be based purely, or even largely, on the
     quantity of money, and rate at which that money circulates
     within the economy — it has done little or nothing to
     reduce prices, but has had a disastrous effect on growth
     and jobs." Combined with an inadequate government adjust-
     ment policy, workers in developed countries reject out-of-
     hand, proposals for structural changes even when essential
     for industrialization in developing countries as well as
     the overall state of economic growth in their own countries.
     Mr Dorrell illustrates the importance of this issue by the
     successful adjustment policies implemented by the Dutch
     Government in their textile sector as compared with the
     backward-looking and protectionist stance of the United
     Kingdom.

(6) The whole orientation of strategy in the preceding develop-
     ment decades may have been misplaced. Both Messrs Jolly
     and Weiss note the failure of the Rostow-type approach to
     DDI when self-sustaining growth after 'take-off' failed to
     materialise, and the growing realisation that something is

fundamentally wrong with the international trade, monetary
and financial systems. Something is also wrong with the
operation of a market system in a world of unequal partners.
There exist deep structural and international defects and
built-in obstacles to progress in the global economy, which
demand fundamental change rather than simple reform.

THE PRESCRIPTIONS

The most important prescriptions for action to meet the challenge of development in the Eighties proposed by the contributors result from their diagnoses of the major obstacles to
success encountered in preceding development decades.

(1) There is a call for a substantial increase in capital
     flows to developing countries, especially the poorest. As
     a minimum, most contributors call for all Governments to
     comply with the 0.7 per cent of GNP target for official
     aid. Mr Marten, the present Minister of Overseas Develop-
     ment, explains that while planned aid expenditures have
     had to be reduced as part of his Government efforts to
     combat inflation, he hopes that when the British economy
     is healthier aid will again increase. He and Mr Dorrell
     stress the importance of encouraging private financial
     flows, which already provide the bulk of external financial
     needs of the middle-income developing countries. Financial
     markets, particularly the City of London financial
     institutions, should continue to be of major importance in
     recycling the surplus revenues of oil producers. Given
     their performance to date, socialist countries should
     expand significantly their aid and financial transfers to
     developing countries.

(2) The rules and principles governing international trade
     must be altered to restructure the international division
     of labour in order to accommodate the growing industrial
     potential andchanging comparative advantage of developing
     countries, including the primary commodity and service
     sectors. Mr Marten observes that despite world-wide
     economic problems both rich and poor agreed that protec-
     tionism was no answer to world recession during GATT multi-
     lateral trade negotiations and UNCTAD V. He is also
     optimistic even regarding liberalisation of the European
     Community's trade policy. While other contributors are
     considerably less sanguine about the existence of protec-
     tionistic pressures, they all nonetheless argue strongly

for creative thinking and new policy measures. Both the
trade and aid possibilities of the first two Lomé Conventions — between the members of the EC and over fifty
developing countries of Africa, the Caribbean and the
Pacific — were particularly emphasized by Mr von Hellsdorff.

(3)   The multinational corporation is seen by Mr Durham as the
principal means through which one can channel to the
developing countries necessary technology, the ability to
manage available resources, marketing skills and distributive capabilities. While he does not dwell upon the well-
known problems of control and abuse of power that are
criticized by other contributors, he nonetheless argues
effectively for greater reliance on the private sector and
less upon international bureaucracies.

(4)   The trade unions, in the view of Mr Jones, should play a
vital role in making North-South issues more open and clear
to working people in order to provide a 'grass-roots'
impetus for changes in policy. The expertise in technical
and trade training schemes, appropriate technology, worker
consultations, co-operatives, and safety standards could
be made available quickly to developing countries by the
trades unions of developed countries.

(5)   Both Mr Marten and Mr Wright are agreed that a strong
domestic economy would provide a good base for responding
to the challenge of development in the Eighties. Unfortunately, the UK economy has, in 1981, unemployment unparal-
leled since the 1930s and high inflation. Government with
an eye on voters and trade unions with an eye on workers,
will inevitably face difficulties in accepting adjustments
to necessary structural changes being called for by developing countries. Nonetheless, difficult and unpopular
decisions need to be taken which require a forward-looking
vision and adequate compensation for displaced workers in
traditional industries like textiles, steel and shipbuilding. Unfortunately, the contributors have little to offer
to escape this impasse. Mr Dorrell advocates a package of
measures and sees no contradiction in a Conservative Government's engaging in planning, although he does not think
that central government can create very many jobs in
comparison with the private sector. Mr Wright advocates
building up and adapting the traditional mix of demand and
supply management, in the context of co-ordinated national
economic strategies.

(6) A fundamental issue is whether or not it is worthwhile to
     formulate an international development strategy for the
     decade. Even those most closely involved with the articu-
     lation of strategies for the first two United Nations
     Development decades have begun to question their utility.
     Professor Jolly, while noting the limitations, argues that
     previous strategies have raised global awareness of develop-
     ment issues, identified and clarified issues in the course
     of their preparations and provided a yardstick to measure
     performance. He concludes that the new IDS is, in the
     final analysis, useful. In the absence of an International
     Development Strategy, certain crucial development issues
     would not be dealt with, while those tackled would be on
     an *ad hoc*, haphazard basis.

(7) The new International Development Strategy, debated at the
     1980 Eleventh Special Session of the UN General Assembly
     and adopted during its 35th regular session, calls for
     radical changes in trade, money and finance, economic co-
     operation among developing countries, relations with the
     most disadvantages countries, food and energy, in order to
     achieve a more equitable and international economic system
     in the Eighties. Mr Weiss notes that although 'reform'
     may be a mere congenial concept to the Western mind then
     'revolution', the transformations called for in the new
     IDS — and necessary to put the global economy on a sound
     and just basis — require "an upheaval in long-established
     expectations and behaviour patterns."

CONCLUSION

It is for readers to judge, having weighed the various contributions to this book from the different interest groups represented, whether society will respond positively and successfully to
the challenge of development in the Eighties. Shifts in the
balance of power among institutions in society — state, church,
capital, labour — and changes in institutions themselves are
desirable and inevitable if growth is to occur. It may be that
a decade is too short a time for significant changes to occur.
Alternatively, if many of the warnings set out by the contributors have substance, then the responses of each interest group
to the challenge of development in the eighties may affect
its institutional structure and nature.

Even if mutual survival is not at stake in the next ten years,
the needless deaths of innocent people that occur daily are a

condemnation of society, undermining the very basis upon which it is built and destroying the vision of what humankind is ultimately about. A variety of responses to the challenges of development in the 1980s are not only possible but also are necessary. The only unacceptable responses are self-satisfaction and inaction.

Index